BRITAIN IN OLD PHOTOGRAPHS

MANCHESTER ROAD & RAIL

EDWARD GRAY

ALAN SUTTON PUBLISHING LIMITED

Alan Sutton Publishing Limited
Phoenix Mill • Far Thrupp • Stroud
Gloucestershire • GL5 2BU

First published 1996

British Library Cataloguing in Publication Data
A catalogue record for this book is available from the
British Library.

ISBN 0-7509-1172-7

Typeset in 10/12 Perpetua.
Typesetting and origination by
Alan Sutton Publishing Limited.
Printed in Great Britain by
Ebenezer Baylis, Worcester.

The power of steam – rebuilt 'Royal Scot' number 46155 *The Lancer* at Patricroft Motive Power Depot in the late 1950s. (J.R. Carter)

CONTENTS

Manchester's Deansgate, 1890. Crowds watch with interest whilst policemen and passers-by attempt to restore a de-railed horse-tram to the tracks near St Mary's Gate. (J.W. Hadfield)

INTRODUCTION

The Manchester region has a long tradition of transport innovation. Three hundred years ago, as the population grew and the former cottage industries began to be concentrated in mills and factories, better means of communication became increasingly necessary. From 1724 the old pack-horse roads were improved by the turnpike trusts, which kept the surfaces in good repair in return for the privilege of charging tolls. The Mersey & Irwell Navigation Company dredged and widened the rivers, and constructed locks to enable boats to reach Manchester by 1734, and by 1761 the Duke of Bridgewater's canal was carrying coal from Worsley to Manchester. The Duke's success encouraged similar schemes. Although the canals did not increase the speed of travel, they offered a cheap means of transport for bulk cargoes, which were difficult and costly to carry by road.

Most people then lived within walking distance of their place of work, and transport improvements were intended to speed the passage of goods rather than people. Even so, long-distance stage-coaches were running from 1754, there were many regular daily services by 1800, and in 1810 the first hackney carriages began to ply for hire in the town centre. Rich merchants moved to homes in the outskirts, and in 1824 John Greenwood, keeper of the toll-gate at Pendleton, observing the regular traffic to and from Manchester's business centre, established the country's first omnibus service. Greenwood's 'sixpenny omnibuses' were soon to be seen on several main roads. The 1830 Liverpool & Manchester Railway, intended mainly for the carriage of goods, offered passenger services. The Manchester to Bolton Railway followed in 1838, and the railway mania of the 1840s saw Manchester at the hub of a network of schemes. The railways soon captured the long-distance passenger traffic, and took over much of the commercial goods traffic from the canals, for they could carry loads much more quickly, though not more cheaply.

In the second half of the nineteenth century, passenger traffic on the roads tended to be confined to short local journeys. Horse-drawn omnibuses proliferated from 1850 onwards, and John Greenwood, Junior, inheriting his father's business, gave the region its first 'tramway' in 1861. He sought to give passengers a smoother ride over the cobble stones by adapting the railway principle to the road, and running omnibuses on rails laid flush with the road surface. The wheels of the omnibus were kept on the rails by means of a central guide wheel, running in a slot. Greenwood's Pendleton to Manchester tramway remained in use until 1872, but the invention of the grooved rail made the guide wheel principle obsolete. The 1870 Tramways Act empowered local authorities to construct lines, which had to be leased to independent operators, and the period from 1877 to 1900 became the era of the horse-drawn tramcar, dominated in the greater part of the region by the Manchester Carriage & Tramways Company. At first, any length of journey cost 3d, but the introduction of graduated charges in 1888 saw the penny fare offered for the first time, thus ushering in a period of cheap local travel. Not for nothing was the tramcar dubbed the poor man's carriage. Britain's largest steam tramway was established in the Bury, Rochdale, and Oldham districts from 1883, though the use of steam-power on the roads was hampered by regulations designed to protect other road users, and involved costly additions to the locomotive to prevent the emission of smoke and steam.

In 1872 railway interests formed the Bridgewater Navigation Company and acquired both canal and river navigation routes to Liverpool. The dissatisfaction of Manchester merchants with the high rates charged by the railway company 'rings', coupled with port dues levied on goods trans-shipped at

Liverpool, led to the construction of the 36-mile-long Manchester Ship Canal. After initial difficulties in gaining Parliamentary approval and raising funds, the Ship Canal was completed in 1894, enabling ocean-going vessels to bring in raw materials and export manufactured goods from a newly created inland port nearer to the factories, thus cutting the costs of transport. The acquisition in 1896 of Trafford Park, alongside the terminal docks, for development as the country's first industrial estate, brought additional transport facilities in the shape of gas-powered tramcars to carry workers to the new factories, the construction of new rail connections, and the establishment of firms producing railway and tramway equipment.

The 1870 Act contained provision for compulsory purchase of tramway assets by the local authority after 21 years. Towards the end of the century this clause held back progress in a disastrous manner, for tramway lessees were reluctant to invest in improvements or conversions when purchase at scrap value was threatened. The early years of the twentieth century saw the fragmentation of the horse-tramway system as local authorities exercised these powers. Councils in the Manchester area agreed to construct electric tramways on the same gauge and to adopt the same method of current collection, so that cross-city routes and inter-running arrangements would be possible from the outset. In fact, municipal jealousies soon created artificial barriers. Tramway undertakings were required to pave and repair the streets between the tracks and for 18 inches either side. On double-track routes, this meant most of the roadway. This was an astonishing burden left over from horse-tram legislation, intended to compensate for wear of the road surface by horses' hooves. But the electric tram ran only on the rails! Tramways also paid rates on the value of the track. Rival motor buses, which did wear out the road surface, suffered no such handicaps. The widespread application of the pneumatic tyre in the mid-1920s, and the advantage of more flexible routing, helped promote the bus and hasten the decline of the tramways. The costs of renewing worn-out track and replacing ageing fleets, led most undertakings to curtail tramway operation in the 1930s and to plan total abandonment. The truncated remains of several systems enjoyed a temporary reprieve in 1939, surviving only until replacement motor buses became available in the immediate postwar years. Electricity continued to power trolley buses for some years longer, but began to be used more extensively on the railways, which were nationalised in 1948. A Passenger Transport Authority absorbed 13 separate road transport undertakings in 1969. Many of the cross-city routes begun in the 1950s were divided at the town centre, terminating either in or around Piccadilly, or in the gloomy and depressing Arndale bus station. The monopoly was broken by 'de-regulation' of bus services in 1987, and the company (now GM Buses) has since been split and privatised, but the familiar pattern of services was lost.

Tramways re-appeared in 1992 with the opening of the first phase of the Metrolink system – an undoubted success, but useful mainly to passengers who live within reach of stations on the former railway routes to Bury and Altrincham. The consortium responsible, which included representatives of Manchester City Council (slogan 'Defending Jobs'), chose to purchase vehicles, rails, bridgework, etc., even street shelters, from the Continent. Only the electric motors and control gear, and some signalling equipment, are of British manufacture. A critic likened this to 'importing unemployment'.

On the main line railways, the opening of the Windsor Link and a line to the airport has given new stations to Salford Crescent and the air terminal, but others have been closed, run down, or left unstaffed. Like it or not, most 'customers' (as the railways currently call their passengers) are now taken to Piccadilly station. The rolling stock provided for many 'trains' is often merely an overcrowded and inadequate two-coach 'sprinter' unit.

On the roads, Greater Manchester Buses continue the confusion made of de-regulation (changes of service numbers, termini, etc.) with frequent alterations to routes and timetables. The management persists in the strange belief that passengers do not mind whether or not a correct service number is displayed on the rear of buses. The former Piccadilly bus station was replaced in 1995 by a new 'interchange' (in transport jargon, that means different bus stands on the same site) with more re-routing 'to eliminate many cross-city centre movements'. But lessons of the past are not heeded. Passengers, particularly if encumbered with baggage, do not wish to change vehicles, nor pay twice for the privilege, and the division of through routes does nothing to reduce the number of vehicles in town centres. Meanwhile, passengers are fewer, private cars continue to flood into the city, taxis and mini-cabs prosper, and transport chiefs wonder why!

HORSE-DRAWN
TRANSPORT

After early competition, omnibus proprietors combined in 1865 to form the Manchester Carriage Company, which offered services along main roads radiating from the city centre to the suburbs. Horse-drawn omnibus L 5, on the Palatine Road to Cheadle service in South Manchester, waits outside the aptly named Horse & Farrier inn, Gatley.

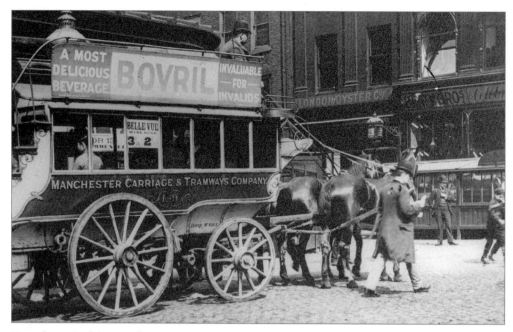

Horse-bus L 9 of the Manchester Carriage & Tramways Company at Market Place (near Victoria Street) Manchester in the 1890s, before commencing its journey via Hyde Road to Belle Vue. Belle Vue Zoo and amusement park was once a noted pleasure ground for Mancunians. The card in the window announces fares of 3d inside or 2d on the open top.

Manchester and Salford councils co-operated in the construction of a tramway from Pendleton to Higher Broughton via Deansgate. Opened in 1877, it was leased originally to Messrs Busby and Turton, who purchased 30 double-ended vehicles built by the Starbuck firm of Birkenhead. Other lines were opened in the 1878–83 period. This is horse tram P 4 at Eccles station in 1879.

Manchester's Deansgate, 1880s. Horse-drawn omnibuses and tramcars mingle, as a Starbuck car prepares to reverse. Two horses for the tram, but three for the omnibus, indicate the relative effort required to haul vehicles over smooth rails as against uneven cobbles. Note the top-deck 'knifeboard' seats. All three nearer vehicles are on duty for cricket at Old Trafford.

The lease of the horse-tram system was transferred to the Carriage Company, which already worked it for the original lessees. In 1877 John Eades, manager of the Pendleton works, patented a shorter, lighter, reversible tramcar, whose body was able to swivel on its truck without the need to unhitch the horses. This is Eades car O 95 – the 'O' indicated its home depot of Openshaw.

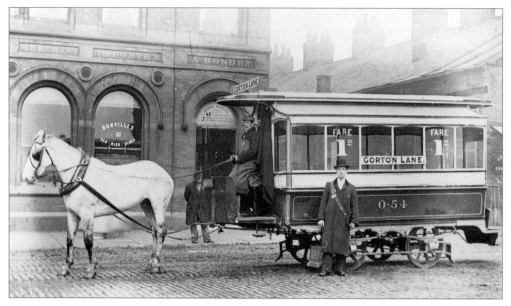

Car O 54, Ashton Old Road. Over 500 Eades patent reversible cars were built at the Company's works. Single-deck versions, seating 16 and pulled by only one horse, were introduced in 1888 to supplement services on inner-city portions of longer routes. In the same year, short-distance 1*d* fares became available for the first time.

An unusual opportunity to view a procession of horse trams was provided by the Blackley Sunday Schools combined outing in hired tramcars. Most are of the Eades reversible type, but the two nearer vehicles are examples of the more austere non-reversible 'workmen's cars', whose top deck was reached via an iron ladder.

In Bolton, a separate tramway system was leased to Edmund Holden, who from 1880 worked on seven routes from the town centre. As in Manchester, destinations painted on the sides of the cars restricted their use to one route only. Car F 5 (the letter F indicating its home depot, Farnworth) is an Eades reversible type. Many were built under licence in other towns.

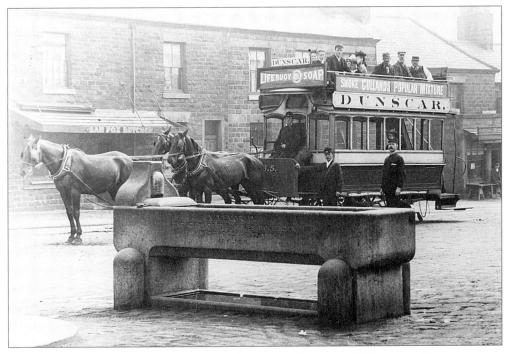

As the Bolton system grew, Holden's eventually owned 48 trams and 350 horses. The horses were changed several times per day, so a considerable stud was required for each tramcar. Depending on gradients, double-deck cars could be hauled by two or three horses. Car B 5 is on Blackburn Road, Dunscar, in 1898. The stone horse trough was a regular feature at road junctions.

In central Manchester, in order to avoid rotating Eades reversible cars in the busy streets, the terminal portions of routes passed around either Piccadilly, or as here, the Victoria Buildings at Exchange. Cars arrived via Victoria Street, but departed via Deansgate. Car H 76, from the Hulme Depot, waiting to leave for Stretford, is followed by cars for Weaste and Greenheys.

Market Street, Manchester, 1889. A Brooks's Bar tramcar (left) moves towards Piccadilly, whilst the cars on the right, having reversed their destination boards prematurely, approach the Exchange terminus. Services were arranged so that some cars from each route would travel the length of Market Street, whilst others would terminate in Piccadilly. (F. Frith)

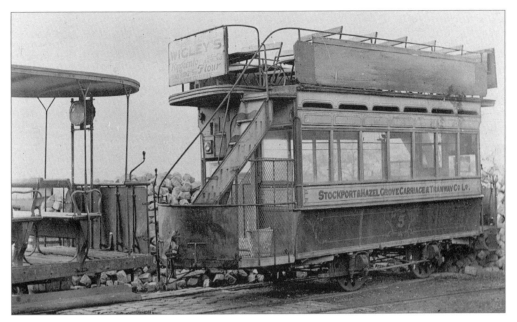

Stockport was connected to Manchester by horse tramway in 1880, the through journey costing 4*d*. Ten years later, the independent Stockport & Hazel Grove Carriage & Tramways Company opened a line to Hazel Grove and a branch to Edgeley. Double-ended car 5 stands with an open-sided 'toastrack' car behind the depot on Wellington Road South.

The Stockport & Hazel Grove Company also operated Eades reversible cars. No. 4 is seen at the Hazel Grove terminus by the Bull's Head Hotel. On the later cars, forward-facing seats on the top deck replaced the old 'knifeboards'. The guard carries a ticket punch machine, evidence of the later years of operation.

The Stockport & Hazel Grove Company eventually owned 20 tramcars, 16 double-deck and 4 single-deck. A single-deck car is here on the Edgeley route. Its number, H 70, suggests that it was purchased second-hand from the Manchester Carriage Company in about 1901.

Horse-tram proprietors had to maintain stables and depots at several points on the system. Such premises were often situated at the outer ends of routes, convenient for early morning journeys to the city centre. The Stretford Depot, by the Old Cock Hotel at the extremity of the line, was photographed in 1901. It remains much the same today, though adapted for other uses.

Local-authority tramways were leased to the operator for a period of 21 years at an annual rent equalling 10 per cent of the cost of construction, and the lessees were therefore the big companies. Other proprietors continued in business in a small way. This all-male outing to Altrincham was in a waggonette owned by Robert Leech, of Queens Road Mews, Cheetham Mill, Manchester.

Market Street, 1902, with a new electric car (centre) amidst the horse-drawn vehicles. The 1870 Tramways Act having been amended to permit municipal operation, the Carriage Company was given notice that leases of the lines would not be renewed. By arrangement, the horse-tram services were continued whilst Manchester converted to electric traction. (Manchester City Engineer)

Eades car L 68 from the Longsight Depot, Rusholme, 30 November 1903. For over two years, horse-trams and electric trams could be seen sharing the tracks whilst the work of converting the system proceeded route by route. The last horse-tram in Manchester ran in 1903, by which time the Carriage Company's empire had dwindled.

Manchester Corporation purchased several horse-drawn omnibuses from the Carriage Company in order to maintain services in outlying districts where it was not thought worthwhile to invest in tramway track construction. Three-horse omnibus no. 9 is seen in corporation livery, complete with civic coat-of-arms and uniformed crew, working the Cheadle route. (MCT)

RAILWAYS IN THE PRE-GROUPING ERA

The 1830 Liverpool & Manchester Railway was the first steam-hauled passenger line in the area, but the Bolton to Leigh Railway had opened in 1828 (for freight only until 1831), using a mixture of steam and horse-power. The Bolton to Salford line opened in 1838, and as railway mania spread, Manchester was approached from several directions. Main line termini were constructed as near as possible to the city centre, which resulted in a ring of stations from London Road, through Oxford Road, Central, Salford, and Exchange, to Victoria. Lines constructed by the Manchester, Sheffield & Lincolnshire Railway (later the Great Central) and the London & North Western Railway (LNWR) reached London Road in 1842, giving the city its first major terminus, joined in 1849 by the Manchester South Junction & Altrincham Railway (MSJ&AR) extension from Oxford Road. The imposing building was erected in 1865, and bore on its canopy names of several destinations served. (Photomatic)

Manchester's London Road station in London & North Western Railway days. The LNWR adopted a policy of fixing brass nameplates on the driving wheel splashers of its passenger engines. No. 40, *Niagara*, a 4–4–0 Precursor class locomotive dating from the 1904–7 period, blows off excess steam as it prepares to depart with a London express. (Real Photographs)

The Great Central Railway evolved from the Manchester, Sheffield & Lincolnshire Railway when that company extended its line to London in 1900. Unlike some other companies, it did not choose to give names to its express engines. Locomotive no. 52 heads a train for Sheffield at Guide Bridge, a focal point of lines in east Manchester, pre-1914. (Real Photographs)

Exchange station, named after the nearby Cotton Exchange, was opened by the LNWR in 1884 to relieve congestion in Victoria, which it shared with the Lancashire & Yorkshire Railway Company (L&Y). The station approach spanned the River Irwell from a point which became the 'Exchange' terminus of many tram routes. (F. Frith)

Exchange station provided additional platforms for the exclusive use of the LNWR. After 1929, when Platform 3 (right) was connected to Platform 11 at Victoria, it boasted the longest continuous platform in Europe. The notice on the barrier reads 'Tickets & Contracts Must Be Shewn When Passing The Barrier'.

Victoria station, looking towards Exchange, 1912. The headquarters of the L&Y since 1844, Victoria had a number of interesting appendages, including a model railway layout for the training of signalmen, and this overhead device to enable the precariously perched operator to transfer parcels between platforms. (National Railway Museum)

At the start of the twentieth century, the Horwich Works (Bolton) of the L&Y built a series of 4–4–2 locomotives which were the most powerful to be seen on a British railway at that time. No. 1412, new in 1902, is seen leaving Victoria and passing the side of the LNWR Exchange station. Unlike the LNWR, the L&Y did not name its main line engines.

Newton Heath Motive Power Depot, north-east of Victoria station, opened in 1876 and was the largest on the L&Y system, having 24 roads to stable and service an allocation of some 200 locomotives. Nos 655 and 688 were two of a series of 40 0–6–2 tank engines designed to cope with heavy local passenger trains, built for the L&Y by the Glasgow firm of Dubs in 1882.

Central station, Manchester, grew from a temporary terminus in 1877 to this grand 1880 building, with the names of the Great Northern, Great Central, and Midland companies prominently displayed. The Cheshire Lines Committee originated from a joint attempt of 1862 to break into LNWR territory and compete for traffic to Liverpool and Chester. (Wyman)

Midland Railway locomotive 768 heads a train at Manchester Central station, from where London-bound expresses followed the scenic Peak District route to St Pancras. The early 1920s saw a period of severe coal shortages, during which several engines were adapted to burn oil. Number 768 was one so equipped – note the oil storage tank on the tender. (Real Photographs)

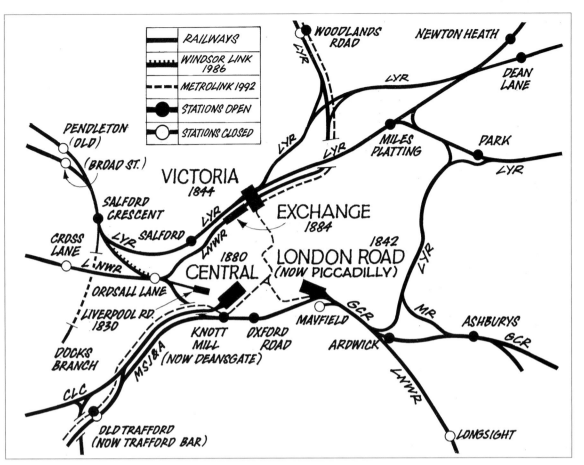

Map showing the location of main line stations in central Manchester, with dates of opening, 1842–84. The main termini ringed the older built-up area in the city centre, and because of the problems involved when passengers had to transfer to trains in a different station, there were several abortive schemes to connect them by underground railway. Motor buses eventually linked London Road (Piccadilly) with Central, Exchange, and Victoria stations, a service which survived into modern times as the 'Centreline' route. With the closure of Exchange and Central stations in 1969, the need remained to link Piccadilly with Victoria, which is now accomplished by a branch of the 'Metrolink' tramway. The construction of the Windsor Link in 1986 enabled trains from the north to reach Piccadilly (or at least two platforms of it) via the now over-used Oxford Road line. Unhappily, it has also permitted Victoria station to be sadly run down. The 1992 'Metrolink' Light Rapid Transit system is shown alongside the former L&Y and MSJ&AR lines (to Bury and Altrincham respectively), which it links by a short section of city centre street tramway. (Map: Alan Palmer)

Barton Moss station, 1887. In contrast to the busy city centre stations, Barton Moss, between Astley and Patricroft on the notorious Chat Moss section of the 1830 Liverpool & Manchester line, was merely a country halt, serving scattered farms. The first station here opened in 1842, being replaced in 1862 by the one illustrated, re-sited east of the original. It closed in 1929.

Clifton Junction, pre-1912. The 1838 Manchester to Bolton Railway was joined in 1846 by the East Lancashire Railway from Bury (right), both absorbed by the L&Y. A third line, for mineral traffic only, was constructed by the LNWR in 1850, passing beneath the Bolton line to join the Bury branch. Since 1966 only the Bolton line has survived. (Barrett)

Worsley station, looking to Monton, 1890. Opened in 1864 on the LNWR's new line from Eccles to Tyldesley, the station remained in use for just over a century, closing when the line was abandoned in 1969.

Walkden (Low Level) station, 1911. The LNWR's new branch to Bolton saw the establishment of this halt in 1875, but a second station (High Level), only a few yards away, opened in 1888 on the L&Y's rival route. The locomotive is an 0–6–2 tank engine and the carriages are in the 'plum and spilt milk' livery, officially designated carmine lake and white.

Moorside & Wardley station, on the L&Y's new 1887 route to Liverpool, remains in use today. The buildings of the island platform, situated between the slow lines, were remarkably substantial for such an area, having separate ladies' and gentlemen's first and second class waiting rooms. In the foreground are the fast lines for non-stop trains. (H. Grundy)

Miles Platting station, east of Victoria on the way to Newton Heath locomotive depot, had a rather unprepossessing approach from Queens Road, but advertised its presence in large letters on the bridge. The Railway Inn (just visible on the left) boasted a concert room, whilst the Station Tavern (right) countered with 'Special Invalid Stout'. A single-deck tramcar approaches in the distance.

East of Manchester, L&Y, GC and LNW lines met at Stalybridge, where 'Claughton' no. 154 *Captain Fryatt* (named after the executed master of a railway-owned ship which sank a German submarine in 1916) heads a Liverpool–Scarborough train. The 'Claughtons' were the last express engines designed for the LNW, 130 being built between 1913 and 1921. (Real Photographs)

Manchester's first railway station on Liverpool Road (1830–44) closed to passengers on the extension of the line into Victoria. Thereafter it reverted to Goods-only use, trains approaching from Ordsall Lane across this original bridge over Water Street. The station site, buildings and associated warehouses are now part of the Greater Manchester Museum of Science & Industry.

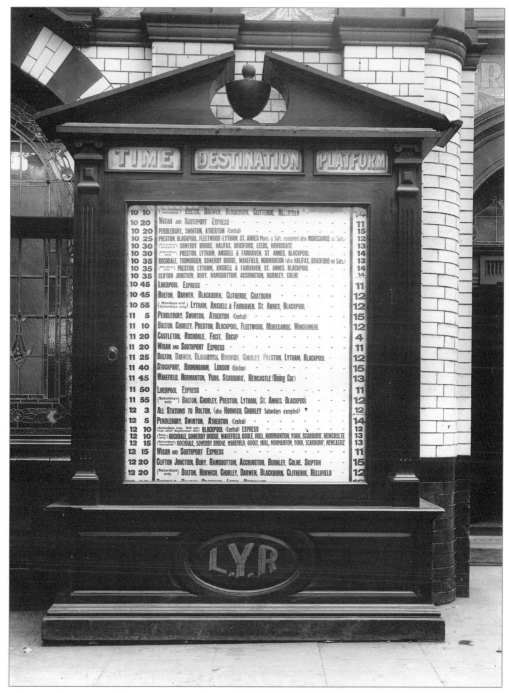

This L&Y departure indicator at Victoria listed mainly the long-distance trains from platforms 11 to 15. Station staff had the task of winding the destination blind at regular intervals. Local stopping trains left from lower-numbered bay platforms. In the middle of the day, there were approximately 12 long-distance departures per hour. (National Railway Museum)

WHAT MIGHT HAVE BEEN — LATE NINETEENTH-CENTURY EXPERIMENTS

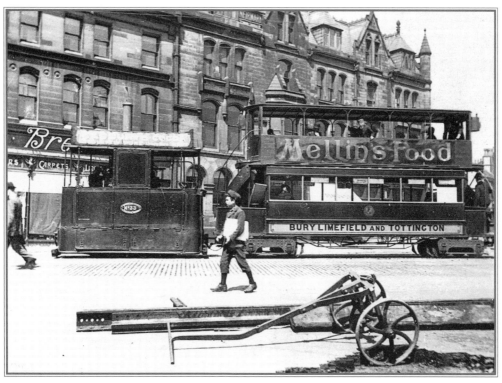

Towards the end of the nineteenth century, when it was clear that horse-drawn traction was about to be superseded, there were several attempts to determine the best form of replacement. Steam-power had been in use on the railways for some considerable time before it was adapted for road haulage. The Manchester, Bury, Rochdale & Oldham Steam Tramways Company (MBRO) was formed optimistically in 1882, but its schemes for a great network of steam-tram services were foiled by existing lessees of lines to Manchester, and handicapped by choosing to work on two different gauges. Steam-tram locomotive 33 (built by Thos Green of Leeds in 1883) is seen with a Falcon-built trailer in Market Place, Bury, working the narrow gauge Bury–Limefield–Tottington route.

Strict regulations governed the operation of steam locomotives on public roads. Working parts had to be concealed, and there was a ban on the emission of smoke or steam. The result was a box-like vehicle, with, usually, a vertical boiler. MBRO standard gauge no. 84, a Wilkinson's Patent Condensing Locomotive built by Beyer Peacock in 1886, is shown here at Royton Depot in about 1900.

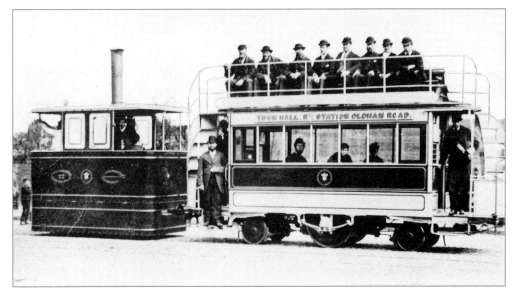

The first steam tramcar in Rochdale was narrow gauge locomotive 22, seen here hauling a small Starbuck-built six-wheeled car, no. 24, at the Dog & Partridge Inn on the Rochdale to Royton section in 1883. The open-top trailer car is unusual in having large-diameter centre wheels.

MBRO narrow gauge engine 49 (Black Hawthorn manufacture of 1884) hauls Falcon eight-wheel trailer 61 on the Littleborough to Royton route. Passengers on the open top deck (with its traditional 'knifeboard' seat) were plagued by smoke, soot and sparks from the locomotive.

In 1889 six 'long car' trailers were constructed by adapting twelve of the small original Starbuck car bodies, and joining them in pairs on new lengthened underframes. The wide centre pillar marks the join. At the same time, top-deck bulkhead ends were fitted to protect passengers from chimney exhaust. The photograph was taken on the Rochdale & Littleborough route in 1897.

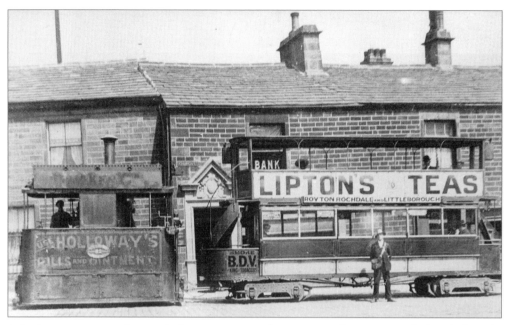

A further improvement for top-deck passengers was the provision of a canopy roof, though the sides remained open and unglazed. The company owned 91 locomotives operating over 30 miles of track. MBRO engine 82 of 1886 with trailer is on the narrow gauge Royton–Rochdale–Littleborough route.

MBRO narrow gauge locomotive 47 with covered top trailer, in rural surroundings at Summit, between Rochdale and Royton. The destinations in this case are painted on the rocker panel, restricting the trailer to the one route. Note the wide mouth of the Hughes patent coupler, an efficient device which remains in use to this day on the Manx Electric Railway.

A Wigan company started a horse-tram service to Pemberton (using Eades reversible cars) in 1880, but steep gradients led to trials with a steam locomotive. By 1882 four engines were hauling the horse trams as trailers, routes to Hindley and Platt Bridge were added, and the change to steam was completed by 1885. Kitson engine 12 with bogie trailer is seen at Pemberton.

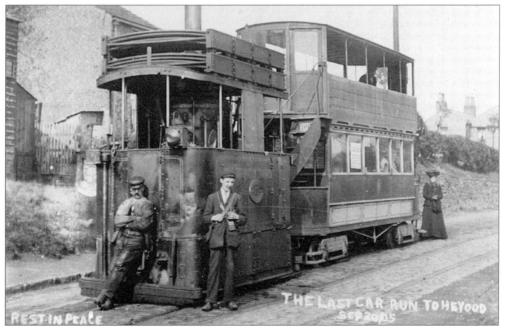

The impending arrival of electric tramways heralded the end of steam on the roads, though Heywood Corporation operated its own short-lived service in 1904–5 when it failed to reach agreement with neighbours Bury and Rochdale, and hastily purchased redundant MBRO vehicles to maintain a service. Engine 81 was the last Heywood steam tram, seen here on 20 September 1905.

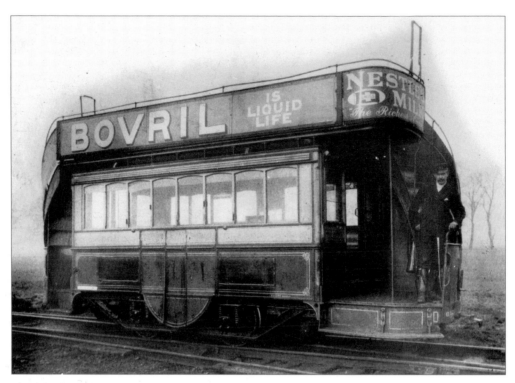

The British Gas Traction Company, formed in 1896 to work tramways on the German Luhrig-Holt system, provided four gas-engined tramcars for the Trafford Park Estates line in 1897–8. The engine, linked to running gear by friction clutches, was powered by ordinary town gas, compressed in a storage tank. Behind the side panels was a large fly-wheel.

Trafford Park Road, 1899. The gas trams ran between Barton and the Old Trafford entrance to the Park, carrying workers to the new factories, but they suffered from the disadvantage of sharing their tracks with goods trains. The 1903 electric tramway displaced them on this part of the route, but the gas cars continued to run at the Barton end until 1908.

Piccadilly, late 1890s. In its peak years, the Carriage Company operated over 500 horse trams on 145 miles of track in the Manchester area, a mixture of municipal and company-owned lines. In 1893 the Municipal Corporations' Association introduced a Bill into Parliament to give local authorities powers to work tramways themselves, powers which had been expressly denied by the 1870 Tramways Act. Municipal ambitions were thus fired, and Manchester and Salford agreed to extend the various 21-year leases of the lines in which they were jointly interested so as to terminate together on 27 April 1901. In fact, the tramways were worked under the jurisdiction of no fewer than 15 separate local authorities, and it was argued that only the company could provide a unified system of public transport in the region. This reasoning proved fruitless, however, and the company faced compulsory purchase of its vast assets at only scrap value. Consequently, the company offered to improve the tramway system, convert it to a new form of traction, and to pay an increased rental from 1901, if renewal of the leases was promised.

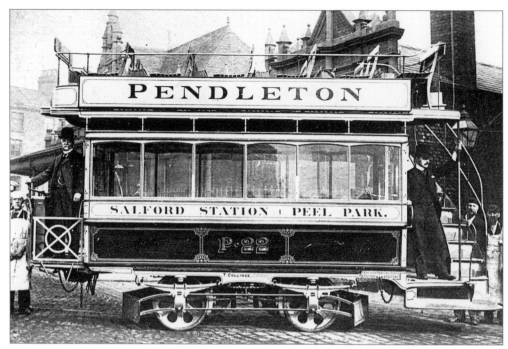

In 1898 the Carriage Company, anxious to prove its capability of adapting to new forms of traction, brought a Serpollet steam tramcar from Paris for demonstration, and John Eades adapted this horse tram to run on electricity, drawing power from storage batteries. In 1899 a sample electric tramcar, built in the company's Pendleton Works, was supplied to Manchester.

The horse-tramway empire crumbled in the face of municipal ambition. The MBRO steam tramway succumbed in similar fashion. A posed picture in Rochdale on 12 May 1905 shows old and new methods of transport. A steam locomotive and trailer, used on the Littleborough route until the day before, stands with one of the new municipal electric tramcars.

ELECTRIC TRAMWAYS, 1899–1920

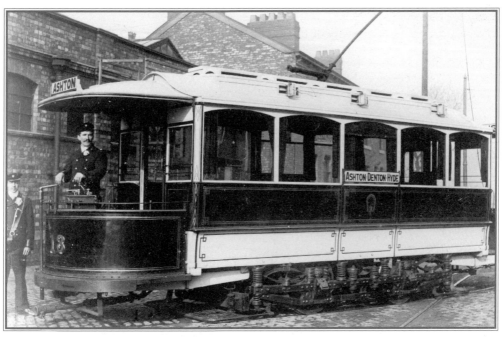

The first electric tramway in the Manchester area was that of the Oldham Ashton & Hyde Company, which had a working life of 22 years before being taken over by larger operators in 1921. It began a service using single-deck 28-seat cars on 12 June 1899. The power supply was provided by Ashton Corporation. In the period 1899–1905, when many towns were preparing for electric traction, the availability of an adequate source of current was a major consideration. Many generating stations were specially built to cater for the increased demand. Car 13 is shown here at Denton Depot, off Ashton Road, in 1899.

Before electric operation commenced, tracks had to be constructed or re-laid, and overhead line equipment had to be installed and connected to a power supply. Bolton Corporation, having bought out the horse-tramway company, commenced its first electric service in December 1899. This was Moses Gate during reconstruction of the Farnworth horse-tram route in 1900.

Although each tramway system maintained its own 'poles and wires' department, skilled and experienced workers were scarce in the early years, and the initial erection of the overhead equipment was often entrusted to specialist firms. George Hill & Co., of Trafford Electric Works, whose horse-drawn tower wagon is seen at Moses Gate, gained several local contracts.

Most smaller local authorities allowed neighbours to work the tramways for them. Bolton provided the first services to Farnworth (Black Horse) in April 1900. Tram 26, bearing only a paper sticker destination indicator, stands at Moses Gate. In 1902, when Farnworth decided to have its own electric tramway, trams terminated here, at the boundary between the two districts.

In the narrow streets of a busy town, single-track with passing places often had to suffice. Bolton tram 32 approaches along Bridge Street, bearing reversible board indicator and a large letter 'H' (for Halliwell). Bolton quickly adopted a system of letters to designate outer destinations. The trolley mast on open-top trams was off-set to allow for the top deck gangway.

In Manchester the Corporation arranged for the Carriage Company to continue horse-tram services until each route was converted for electric traction. Installation of new track for the heavier electric tramcars proceeds at the Oxford Street/Portland Street junction, 1901. Stone road setts stored on the far pavement wait to be reinstated.

Manchester's first electric service, from Albert Square to Cheetham Hill, began on 6 June 1901. Failure to agree terms for Salford cars to run on to Deansgate meant that in return Manchester cars were debarred from part of Bury New Road. Manchester car 298, seen here in Deansgate mixing with horse trams, was operating a temporary service to the boundary at Grove Inn, 1901.

Manchester open-top bogie car 473 was a 1901 Brush product, seating 30 on the lower deck and 39 on top. In the early years, destinations were painted on a four-sided box, which could be rotated to show the correct terminus. An inspector poses on the platform step. Between him and the conductor stands the trolley boy, a third member of crew peculiar to Manchester and Salford.

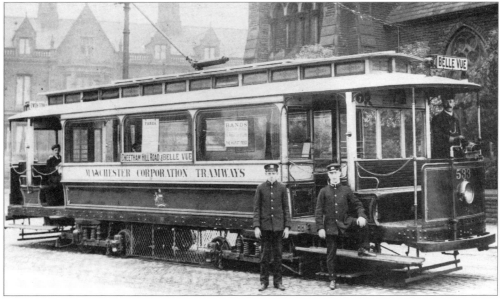

Manchester's circuitous route from Cheetham Hill to Brooks's Bar, which skirted the city centre and passed beneath numerous low bridges, was worked with single-deck cars. Number 533 was a 1903 delivery from Milnes of Birkenhead, successor to the Starbuck Company. Again note the trolley boy, whose duties included the supervision of passengers boarding or alighting.

Salford's dispute with Manchester was solved in 1903, from which time all Salford's routes were arranged to pass along some part of Manchester's Deansgate. Consequently, Salford cars always seemed in the majority on this length of track. Of the eight cars visible in this 1903 postcard, seven are Salford vehicles.

In 1903 Salford was the first to fit an experimental top-cover to an open car. Covered cars were claimed to have higher revenue-earning capacity, because more people would use them in wet weather. Twenty trams were fitted with covers of the type seen on car 98, as it passes one of the new bogie cars at the junction of Bury New Road and Great Clowes Street.

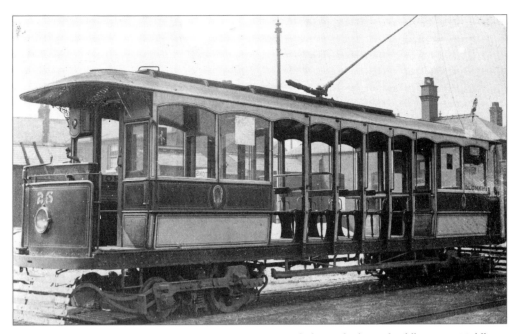

The Middleton Electric Traction Company began a service linking Rhodes and Oldham, via Middleton town centre, in March 1902. Car 25 was a Brush-built single-deck combination car, which was later sold to the Potteries Electric Traction Company. The Middleton Company was taken over by the neighbouring authorities in 1925.

Rochdale Corporation opted to take over the steam tramway within the borough, but as this could not be arranged until 1904, and as the steam lines were laid to the narrow gauge, electric tramcars were first used on entirely separate routes to Bamford and Norden. Car 3, supplied by the Electric Railway & Tramway Carriage Works, Preston, was photographed when new in 1902.

Whilst municipal authorities prepared to run electric tramcar services within their boroughs, the South Lancashire Tramways Company (SLT), centred on Atherton, provided links between various separate undertakings. Its lines filled the gaps in a vast network between Manchester and Liverpool. Car 33, on the Hindley route, was one of 45 bought for the start of services in 1902.

The SLT's Haydock–Hindley section completed a link which enabled a ceremonial through journey to be made from Liverpool Pier Head over five different systems to Bolton in March 1903. Other lengths remained under construction. Stirrup Bridge, Boothstown, was the temporary terminus of the line through Worsley to Swinton and Farnworth in 1905.

The SLT Company built its own power station behind the tramway depot at Atherton. Its lines served some less populous districts, and so did not earn great returns for its shareholders in the early years. Lack of revenue led to an aborted proposal to utilise the lines for freight traffic at night. Car 19, with new roller blind indicator, stands at Mosley Common in 1908.

For two years Bolton provided the electric car service in Farnworth, but in 1902 the local council opened its own tramway, which it hoped would be a vital link on the route to Manchester. Bolton retaliated by refusing to allow Farnworth cars into its territory. Independent operation thus proved unsuccessful, and in 1906 the 13 Farnworth cars were taken over by SLT.

Bolton's wooden boards for destination and route letter displays created problems of issue and storage in the depots, and were soon discarded in favour of roller-blind equipment. Car 12 at the Royal Oak Hotel, Bradshaw Brow, on the Tonge Moor route, carries the new fittings on the top-deck ends, but retains a side route board.

Manchester trams penetrated south-westwards through Stretford into Cheshire, reaching Sale in 1906 and Altrincham in the following year. Car 308 stands at the Sale station terminal stub in School Road, ready to begin its return journey to Piccadilly. Note the large oil lamp on the dashplate.

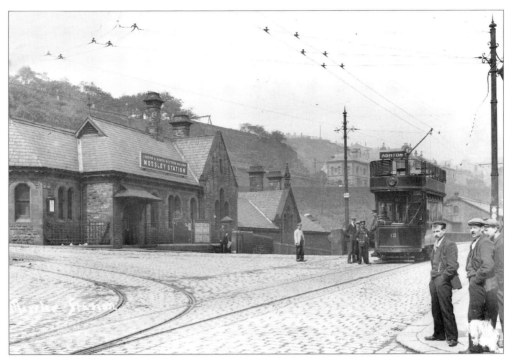

The Stalybridge, Hyde, Mossley & Dukinfield Joint Board (SHMD) was the lengthy title of the undertaking whose tramway served these townships east of Manchester from 1904. Car 12, a Trafford Park product of the British Electric Car Company with Westinghouse equipment, stands outside the LNWR Mossley station in about 1910.

The SHMD Joint Board purchased a number of small single-deck cars, supplied by the same manufacturers, for services passing under low railway bridges. The crew of car 21, destination Acres Lane, Stalybridge, pose for the camera on a rural single-track section of route.

Bury, previously served by both standard and narrow gauge steam trams, commenced electric operation in 1903. Through-running on a joint route to Bolton began in 1907. Bury car 16, at 'Three Arrows' on Bury & Bolton Road in the district of Radcliffe, was one of 12 cars fitted with top covers in 1905–6.

In 1903 Manchester began a programme of fitting top-covers to the open cars. The first covers, known as 'balloons', left the staircase exposed, but were followed by the balcony-type with an extended canopy over the platform. Both forms are seen in this view of Princess Street, c. 1914. (J. Pollard)

After early experiments with a motor bus, Bolton purchased three single-deck tramcars in 1910, specifically for use on the short but steeply graded Darcy Lever route. Seating 38 passengers, these cars served until replaced by motor buses in 1928, Bolton's first tramway abandonment. Route letter 'A' was chosen because 'D' was already in use for Dunscar. (St Regis)

Oldham's electric tramways began in 1900 with single-deck and open-top cars. By 1911 new orders were for cars already fitted with a balcony-type top-cover. Car 94, seen at the Star Inn junction, was supplied by the United Electric Car Company of Preston in 1913.

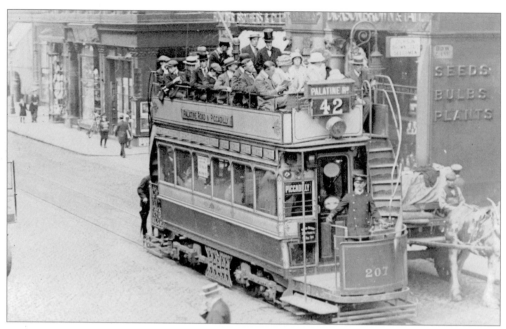

Manchester introduced route numbers in 1914. Stencil plates slotted into holders over opaque glass, and, illuminated from behind at night, supplemented the roller-blind destinations and side route boards. Well-loaded bogie car 207 passes along Cross Street in about 1915–16. (J. Pollard)

Deansgate, Manchester, at its junction with Quay Street and Peter Street, 1921. Manchester's route 10 to Cheetham Hill remained the province of open-top cars because of a low railway arch on Great Ducie Street. Manchester four-wheel car 112 joins a gaggle of Salford cars, as an open motor charabanc leaves Peter Street. (National Railway Museum)

MOTOR BUSES, 1900–1939

The motor bus appeared in the Manchester area early in the twentieth century. At first it was not seen as a competitor to the new electric tramways, but rather as a feeder to them, bringing additional passengers to the main routes, or working in areas where it was not thought worthwhile to construct tramway track. This Manchester-registered example, crowded on both decks, was on a private hire outing.

The first local municipal authority to experiment with the motor bus was Bolton, where in November 1903 a Stirling steam omnibus was tried briefly on the Brownlow Fold–Darcy Lever route. This was returned to the makers, and another more powerful example was tried in September 1904, after which a horse-drawn omnibus returned to the route.

Manchester Tramways chairman, Daniel Boyle, transferred his allegiance to a short-lived Motor Omnibus Company in 1906. In the same year, the Corporation acquired three motor buses to replace the horse-bus services to Northenden and Cheadle. The buses had local Crossley engines in Leyland chassis, with bodies by the tramcar-building firm of Dick Kerr, Preston. (MCT)

The Manchester Carriage & Tramways Company was broken up with the advent of municipal operation of the tramways, but the Company continued as a much-reduced business, offering private hire hansom cabs, waggonettes, and latterly taxis, surviving well into the 1980s. This was one of their first motorised vehicles, a low-capacity bus of 1913.

The South Lancashire Tramways had flirted with motor bus operation in 1906 and again in 1914. In 1919 the Company purchased 25 ex-War Department Dennis chassis with new charabanc or bus bodies, to use as a private hire fleet. This garage view includes charabancs no. 18 (B 8769) in the centre, and no. 3 (B 8667) at the rear.

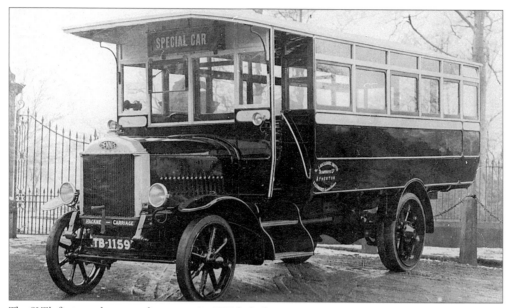

The SLT's first regular motor bus routes in 1920 linked existing tramcar termini at Lowton and Haydock. Other services followed in the Leigh and Golborne area. Atherton Depot was extended to accommodate the growing fleet. Bus 30 (TB 1159) was one of several Dennis 32-seaters purchased in 1920, later fitted with pneumatic tyres.

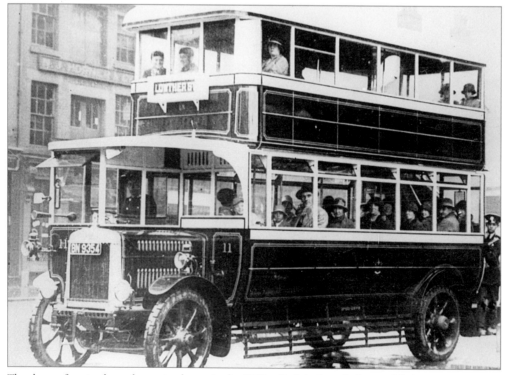

The shape of motor buses began to change in the 1920s. Both body and chassis of Bolton 11, BN 9354, were of Leyland manufacture. Note the solid tyres and oil lamps. The photograph was taken in Victoria Square, Bolton, in 1926. (Leyland Motors)

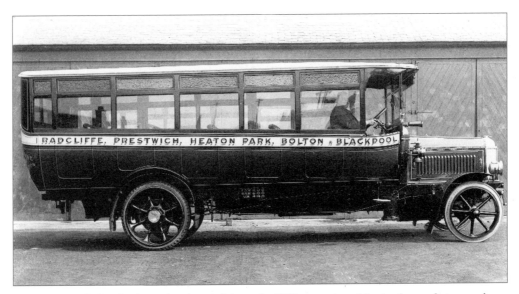

This solid-tyred closed-saloon charabanc of the early 1920s was also of Leyland manufacture and was operated by a Bolton coach proprietor (probably Albert Parry of Mill Street) on long-distance seaside excursions. Note the bulb horn protruding through the cab front, and the outline suggestion of former door placements on the side panels.

The North Western Road Car Company, formed in 1923, made its headquarters in Stockport. Thomas Tilling Ltd held a considerable interest in the Company, and supplied numbers of new vehicles. This solid-tyred example is thought to be a 1926 Tilling Stevens TS4 of the 193–204 series, which remained in service until 1931.

Mersey Square, Stockport, 1925. The crew of a North Western Tilling Stevens bus (number 167, DB 5067) pose for the cameraman during their turn-round time on the Cheadle route. Note the steering column projecting through the cab's front panel. A Stockport tramcar is seen passing behind the bus.

To the south-west of Manchester, Tetlow & Collier commenced omnibus services in the Flixton and Urmston districts. This AEC Renown TD 4054 was new in 1925 and was one of six vehicles taken over when the firm was acquired by the North Western Road Car Company in 1928.

The SHMD Joint Board did not acquire motor buses until 1925. Fleet numbering started at 71 to avoid confusion with the trams. Number 77 (MB 9697) was one of the first batch of eight Thornycroft 26-seaters. The rear door was later disused. Note the 'Tramways' title. The pneumatic tyre did much to advance the popularity of the bus.

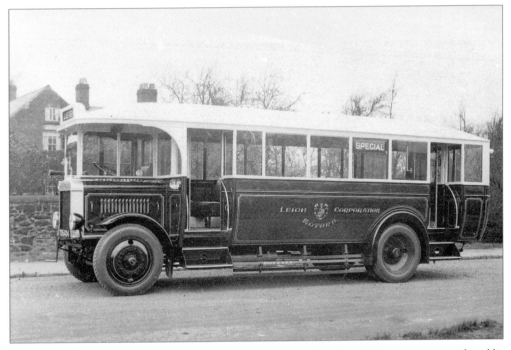

The town of Leigh never had its own trams, being content to allow the SLT Company to provide public transport in its area. However, in 1920, to the dismay of the Company, Leigh began to run its own bus services. Bus 17 (TD 5404), a Leyland PLSCI, was new in 1926. The Leigh livery was always a rich shade of blue. (Leyland Motors)

Wigan Leyland Lion, no. 10 (EK 6043), a 31-seater new in 1928, stands over the puddles and tram tracks of the depot, from which trams had disappeared in 1931. The bus, still carrying the 'Tramways' title, lasted little longer, being withdrawn in 1932. The destination, partly obscured, reads ABRAM, a district of Wigan.

Until 1929 Wigan had only single-deck motor buses. Leyland Titan double-deck bus no. 2 (EK 7260) was one of many bought in 1929–31 for tramway replacement services. The location is Wigan's Market Place. Note Woolworth's 3d and 6d store with the legend 'Nothing over 6d' and the sign for the 'Central station L&NE railway'.

Depot staff at Bolton's Crook Street Garage demonstrate the art of bus washing with power hoses. The bus is a Leyland 'Long Lion' (no. 29, WH 205) of 1927, which remained in service until 1939. The careful lining-out of the front panels and the duplication of the fleet number is well illustrated. (C.E. Willis)

Conversion of the single-deck tram route to Darcy Lever took place in 1928 with a batch of double-deck Leyland vehicles with rear open staircases. Tram wires remain in place as no. 37 (WH 801) climbs from the terminus. The location is the same as in the view of the single-deck tram on page 49. (Leyland Motors)

As the bus routes proliferated, 'Lancashire United' was the name adopted by the motor bus division of South Lancashire Transport. No. 130 (TE 2773) was a Leyland TD1 new in 1928, and, like the Bolton vehicles of the same vintage, had an open-staircase body, with 'piano-front' profile. (Leyland Motors)

Bolton double-deck bus 58 (WH 2602) of 1930, a Leyland TD1 with Roberts body, stands with Ribble and other buses in Victoria Square by the Town Hall in November 1930. Victoria Square ceased to be used as an omnibus stand during the following month. (St Regis)

The Rochdale Canal (through the arch at the end of the side street) was the unlikely starting point for a number of private services which were not licensed to pick up in Manchester streets. A 1929 photograph captures a Blackpool-bound Vanguard Express coach leaving Lena Street to join the main traffic on London Road.

The 'pirate' omnibus operators of the late 1920s were largely squeezed out of local services by municipal undertakings, but those offering long-distance excursions prospered. Auty's of Bury was one such company, here represented by this 1935 picture of an Albion coach.

A 1931 North Western Leyland TD1 with low-bridge body, DB 9398, fleet no. 498, typifies the new shape of the double-deck bus in the early 1930s. The front profile became known as the 'piano front' because of its resemblance to an upright piano. (Leyland Motors)

Kay Gardens, Bury, 9 April 1932. During the Holcombe Hunt point-to-point race meetings, all Bury's available buses, together with many hired from neighbouring authorities, operated a non-stop shuttle service to Ainsworth. Bus 23, left, stands in front of a borrowed Salford low-bridge bus, as vehicles work their way round the triangle.

When Manchester Corporation converted the single-deck tramcar route 53 to motor bus operation in 1930, a total of 60 low-bridge vehicles (20 Crossley and 40 Leylands, with bodies supplied by no fewer than five different builders) were purchased. The conversion was not without its difficulties, for the busy semicircular route crossed major traffic arteries, and minor accidents became commonplace. Bus 239, VR 5758, a Leyland Titan TD1 with Strachan 'piano-front' body, was photographed in 1933 after a collision with a tram pole. (MCT)

Manchester bus 457 (AND 93), a Crossley Mancunian of 1934. Timber-framed bus bodies had not lasted well in continuous service, so builders experimented with metal frames. Accles & Pollock, manufacturers of steel tubing, supplied the frames for the Crossley bodies of the 436–465 batch. (MCT)

Manchester's Piccadilly bus station had grown from small beginnings in 1931 to occupy the whole length of Parker Street. In this 1935 view, looking towards Mosley Street, Oldham and North Western buses mingle with Manchester's own, whilst tramcars (including one from Stockport, top right) skirt the perimeter. (MCT)

Conversion of tramcar routes to motor bus operation continued throughout the 1930s, and the number of buses grew as the tramcar total diminished. In 1937 Bolton purchased 40 new Leyland TD5 chassis to replace trams. Bus 103 (WH 9201) has a Leyland body, whilst that of 118 (WH 9216) is from Massey Brothers of Wigan. (St Regis)

RAILWAYS AFTER 1923

Under the grouping arrangements of 1923, the Midland, LNWR and L&Y railway companies were transferred to the London, Midland and Scottish Railway, which thus assumed control of most, though not all, railways in the Manchester area. The London & North Eastern group absorbed the Great Central, thus sharing occupation of Manchester's London Road station, and certain joint interests (such as the Cheshire Lines Committee) continued to be represented in the region. Patricroft-based ex-LNWR locomotive, renumbered as LMS 8786, leaves the former LNWR Exchange station with a stopping train to Chester. (Locofotos)

Manchester Exchange station in May 1937, with Great Western 'Bulldog' 4–4–0 engine 3212 *Earl of Eldon*. Under joint running arrangements, Great Western engines regularly worked into Manchester on trains from North Wales via Chester. They were serviced at Patricroft engine shed before returning to their home territory.

Third class tickets issued from Manchester Exchange station: (a) Great Western half-day excursion to Llangollen; (b) GWR monthly return to Wrexham; (c) LNWR single to Patricroft; and (d) LMSR reduced fare (for service personnel on leave) to Rainhill. The number 566 on LNW and LMS tickets was the identifying code for Manchester Exchange.

John Aspinall, Chief Mechanical Engineer of the L&Y in 1886, and later its General Manager, was responsible for several successful designs of locomotive. This 0–6–0 goods engine of 1909 was one of many Aspinall products which had a remarkably long life. Seen at Newton Heath Shed in 1931 as LMS 12549, it remained in service until 1961.

A two-coach 'push-pull' local stopping train in charge of an LMS tank engine passes Sanderson's sidings, Roe Green, Worsley. The sidings were used to assemble long trains of coal produced in local collieries. (W.D. Cooper)

A 1935 aerial view of the Manchester Ship Canal near Trafford Bridge shows Pomona Docks (centre top), used by small coastal ships, and part of the extensive dock railway system (bottom left). The narrower Bridgewater Canal (right) is separated from the main canal by only a few yards at one point, the present site of a new lock connecting the two waterways. To the right of

the narrow canal may be seen the triangular Throstle's Nest junction, which connected the Cheshire Lines route between Manchester Central and Liverpool with the Midland route to the south via Didsbury. Above the junction may be seen the Cornbrook carriage sidings, and (top right) the MSJ&AR line near Trafford Bar. (Aerofilms)

The 8½ mile MSJ&AR line between Manchester London Road and Altrincham, although nominally independent, was administered jointly by the LMS and LNER. It was converted to electric operation with car sets supplied by Metropolitan Cammel. This is Oxford Road station on the first day of operation of the new system, 11 May 1931.

The Cheshire Lines Committee was also a joint enterprise. Although the company had its own carriages displaying the CLC title (and staff with CLC cap badges), its trains were hauled by LNER locomotives, an arrangement continued from Great Central practice. Tank engine 5018 takes water at Manchester Central station. (Locofotos)

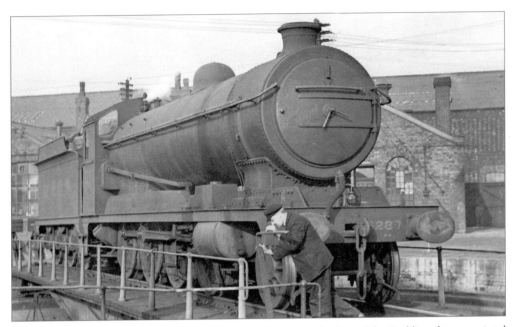

The former Great Central Railway's Gorton Works (known to locals as 'The Tank') and its associated locomotive shed, continued under the LNER group. Close by, but on the other side of the former GC main line, was the Beyer Peacock foundry. This 1939 view shows a grimy 6287 on the engine turntable.

The MSJ&AR lines to Altrincham were used as part of a through route to Chester via Northwich. LMS no. 6, a Fowler-designed 2–6–2 tank engine, arrives at Timperley in 1945. Criticised for their ungainly front-end appearance, 70 such locomotives were built, all being withdrawn in the 1959–62 period. (Locofotos)

LMS 'Royal Scot' 6114 *Coldstream Guardsman* hauls a Manchester to London express under the LNW signal gantry at Longsight in 1947. The 70 locomotives of this class, built 1927–30, were named after regiments. In their original form they were rarely seen in Manchester, but appeared regularly from the late 1940s onwards. (Locofotos)

When the railways were nationalised in 1948, 40000 was added to LMS locomotive numbers. Another rebuilt Scot, 46110 (ex-6110) *Grenadier Guardsman*, arrives in Exchange station in the 1950s with a train from Liverpool. Smoke deflectors were fitted to improve visibility from the driving cab.

Towards the end of the steam era, classes hitherto rostered elsewhere came to be found on workings to Manchester. Arriving beneath the recently installed electrified wires at Piccadilly (formerly London Road) station with a train from London Euston in 1962 is 46250 *City of Lichfield*. At this date 46250's home shed was Carlisle. (Locofotos)

Sir Henry Fowler, Chief Mechanical Engineer first to the Midland and then to the LMSR, designed a powerful medium-sized 2–6–4 tank engine for general passenger duties. Used widely, 125 were built between 1927 and 1934. Ex-LMS 42304 from Longsight shed pauses at the Mauldeth Road box on the former LNW line to Wilmslow.

Sir William Stanier's LMS 'Jubilee'-class engines, of which 191 were built in 1934–6, were the mainstay of the express locomotive fleet in the Manchester area until the mid-1960s. Ex-LMS 'Jubilee' 45698 *Mars* leaves Manchester Victoria with a Newcastle–Liverpool express. (J.R. Carter)

The age of steam was coming to an end in the 1960s, but great quantities of goods were still carried by rail, and elderly work-horses continued to shunt wagons and assemble trains in goods yards up and down the country. Tank engine 47165 was working container traffic in the New Bailey Street yard, Salford, in 1962. (Photomatic)

INDUSTRIAL RAILWAYS

The Manchester area boasted a great number of private railways. The world's first industrial estate, Trafford Park, established in 1896, developed a network of tracks, with connections to the main line railways, to serve the various factory sites. The Trafford Park Estates Company itself owned several locomotives, which worked alongside those of the Manchester Ship Canal Company and those owned by individual firms. This 1906 view of Westinghouse Road includes a Salford Corporation electric tramcar bound for the city centre, and, on tracks alongside, two Ship Canal locomotives (the nearest is no. 18 Savannah) hauling a rake of newly built coaches for export via the nearby docks. (MSCCo)

Bollin was a Hunslet engine of 1889, used by the contractor during the construction of the Ship Canal, and retained (unnumbered) to work for the Canal Company for several years. The locomotive driver and fireman are accompanied by the shunter, carrying a hooked pole for the rapid uncoupling or coupling of wagons when marshalling trains. (MSCCo)

Manchester Ship Canal locomotive no. 28 *Belfast*, a Hudswell Clarke product of 1903, lasted 60 years in Company service. Engines of pre-1914 vintage were named (mostly after ports of the world), but the practice ceased, and later, probably for clerical convenience, numbers only were displayed.

One of the earliest, largest and most important firms to take land in Trafford Park was the British Westinghouse Electrical & Manufacturing Company Limited. This was their 1901 locomotive, built by Manning Wardle of Leeds. Note the large bell behind the chimney, the re-railing jack on the front buffer beam, and the oil lamp.

Turner Brothers locomotive no. 2 hauls a train of Ship Canal wagons carrying steel wheels and axles. Usually factory-owned locomotives would not venture far beyond the works' precincts, traffic between firms or to the docks being handled by engines of the Ship Canal or Estates Company.

Sir William Bailey (named after a director of the Estates Company) was purchased new from Hudswell Clarke in 1908 at a cost of £900, specifically to haul a thrice-daily workmen's train, which replaced the ailing gas tram service to Barton. During the remainder of the day, the engine was employed on general duties.

To make up the workmen's train, the Estates Company bought two second-hand four-wheeled carriages from the Cheshire Lines Company. Tramway-type tickets were issued as passengers boarded. The guard, lacking a uniform, was equipped with cash bag and ticket punch. The carriages are seen here at Barton in 1908.

The Trafford Park workmen's train ceased running in 1921, when it was discovered that regulations governing the Estate railways did not permit any traffic other than goods. Three London-type AEC motor buses (TB 7888–90) were purchased in replacement. In 1925 the Lancashire United Company took over both the buses and the service.

Trafford Park's *Lord Ashburton*, a Hudswell Clarke engine of 1916 named after a director of the Company, was built to the same design as some Ship Canal locomotives. The Company logo was a combined T and P on the side of the coal bunker. The engines were sold in the 1920s, and Park traffic was then handled by Ship Canal locomotives. (TPECo)

Trafford Park Road in the 1930s, with workers returning home at the end of the day. Railway tracks flanked both sides of the road, and penetrated factory gates. In travelling the 2½ mile electric tramway loop in the Park, 34 tramway/railway crossings had to be negotiated, one of which is visible by the lorry.

Timber wagons alongside No. 9 Dock, Salford. The Canal Company operated the largest private railway system in the country. With 75 locomotives and 2,700 wagons, it employed over 790 people. The canal and docksides were flanked with 231 miles of track, enabling cargoes to be transferred direct between railway wagon and ship. (MSCCo)

The region had a thriving locomotive construction industry. Many steam engines were exported via Salford Docks. Beyer Peacock products destined for shipment to Buenos Aires, Argentina, stand on temporary track as they await loading in the late 1920s. (MSCCo)

Fully assembled steam locomotives from the Vulcan Foundry at Newton-le-Willows stand on LMSR well-wagons pending shipment in 1929. Salford Docks were also the outlet for exports from Nasmyth's of Patricroft, and in the 1950s of electric locomotives from Metropolitan Vickers, formerly the Westinghouse. (MSCCo)

Railway carriages built in local factories for overseas customers were regular exports from Salford Docks. Ship Canal locomotive no. 39 *Sydney*, having lost its nameplate, carries a painted title as coaches for Palestinian railways are brought to the dockside in about 1935. (MSCCo)

The Ship Canal Engineer's locomotive, no. 84, a Hunslet saddle-tank of 1932, was often used to haul the cashier's coach. This was a second-hand vehicle of unknown origin, which was used from 1946 to 1953 to pay wages to staff along the canal between Salford and Latchford, a duty which had formerly been undertaken by launch. (C. Cheetham)

The last steam engines ordered by the Canal Company were three Hudswell Clarke saddle-tanks of 1954, numbered 88–90, which served only ten years. No. 90 hauls wagons of imported tobacco across the swing railway bridge to a bonded warehouse on Trafford Wharf. Subsequent orders, from 1959 to 1966, were for diesel locomotives. (MSCCo)

Steam survived longer on the colliery railways in the area to the north-west of Manchester. Eventually absorbed by the National Coal Board, all were connected to mainline tracks. *Sir Robert* (ex-North Staffordshire no. 2 of 1920) and *Wizard*, a post-war saddle-tank, assemble a train of loaded wagons at Sandhole Colliery in 1966. (E. Gray)

With the decline of the coal industry, surviving steam locomotives often remained in use to clean up the area after pits had closed. This was the case at Astley Green in 1970, when saddle-tank locomotives *Stanley* and *Harry* were at work removing waste material and general debris from the surface after mining had ceased. (E. Gray)

Walkden Yard, Worsley, was the National Coal Board's area workshop for the repair and maintenance of steam locomotives. Engines requiring major attention were brought by road from collieries as far away as Cumbria. Awaiting disposal in 1968, were, right to left, *Sir Robert*, *Renown*, *Wasp*, *W.H.R.*, and *Bridgewater*. (E. Gray)

ELECTRIC TRAMWAYS, 1921–1951

A view which epitomises the network of connected tracks in the Manchester region and through-running arrangements, this is the scene at Hyde Market Place in the mid-1930s, where tramcars from Manchester, SHMD and Stockport met. Most tramway systems were substantially complete as early as 1906, and various links between operators meant that there was a physical connection of Lancashire tracks from points as far east as Rochdale, Oldham and Stalybridge to the far west some 40 miles away at Liverpool's Pier Head. However, long-distance tramway services never materialised, much to the disappointment of Liverpool's Manager Bellamy, who favoured them. (W.A. Camwell)

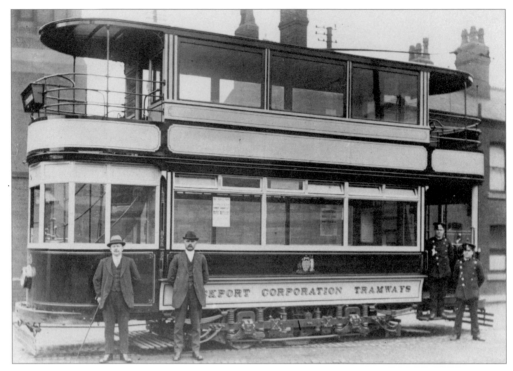

Improvements to tramcar fleets accelerated in the 1920s. Crews objected to the use of open-ended cars, particularly in bad weather. The first Stockport tram to be extensively rebuilt with platform vestibules was no. 29. In this case, the old-style open balconies were retained.

In contrast, Oldham 54 had vestibule ends on both decks. This was one of three tramcars rebuilt to all-enclosed form in 1922–3. It is seen at the terminus of route 9 on Chadderton Road, ready to return to Oldham town centre.

In 1925 Oldham acquired eight single-deck cars (113–120) on the take-over of the Middleton tramways. Originally supplied by the Brush Company in 1899 as trailers for the Oldham Ashton & Hyde sytem, the Middleton Electric Traction Company purchased them in 1903 and converted them to motorised cars.

Despite many improvements in the 1920s, limited funds allocated for reconstruction ensured that many open-ended cars remained in service. The Wigan tramway system closed relatively early, and car 90, keeping open platforms to the end, was in service at Abbey Lakes Pleasure Ground on the last day, a wintry 28 March 1931.

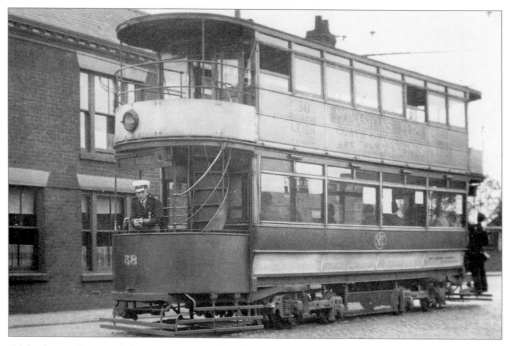

Of the former Farnworth bogie cars acquired by the South Lancashire Tramways in 1906, most were top-covered and rebodied in the mid-1920s. Car 58 was photographed at Four Lane Ends, Over Hulton, working the route to Leigh in 1933, the last year of SLT tramway operation. Eight of these cars were then sold to Bolton. (M.J. O'Connor)

Some open-top tramcars survived into the 1930s. Some, as in Salford, were kept to operate on low-bridge routes, but were fitted with platform vestibules. This Rochdale example lacks such additions, and contrasts with all-enclosed Manchester car 990 on joint route 17 to High Street. The Rochdale tramways closed in 1932. (W. Gratwicke)

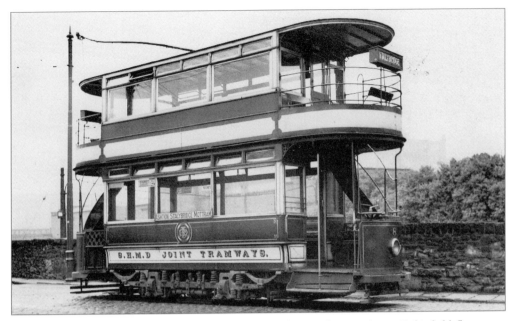

Most of the original open-top tramcars of the Stalybridge, Hyde, Mossley & Dukinfield fleet were improved with the addition of a balcony top-cover from 1912 onwards. Car 8, new in 1904 from the British Electric Car Company of Trafford Park, is seen in 1937. The livery earned the cars the nickname 'green linnets'. (W.A. Camwell)

SHMD balcony cars were virtually indistinguishable from each other, though the last four (61–64), on trucks from Mountain & Gibson of Bury, had been constructed only in 1924–5. Cars used on the joint Hyde to Manchester services carried fittings to display Manchester-style route number plates. Car 51 is at the Exchange terminus in 1935. (A.M. Gunn)

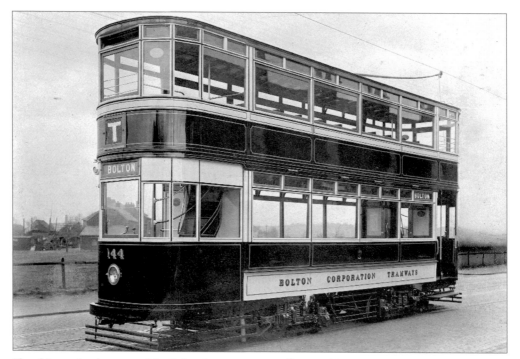

The ultimate development of the Bolton bogie tramcar is illustrated by the clean lines of the all-enclosed body of car 144, supplied new by the English Electric Company in 1927. Seating 29 on the lower deck and 48 on top (total 77, plus standees when necessary), these high-capacity tramcars proved great crowd-movers. (Bolton Transport)

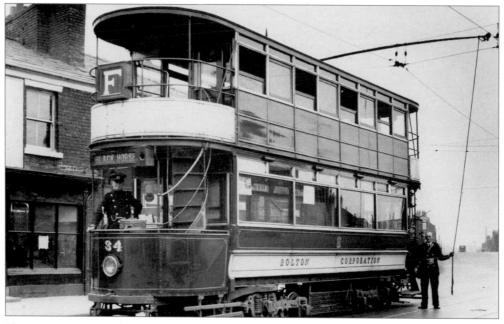

The antique appearance of Bolton's ex-Farnworth cars (acquired from SLT in 1933) contrasted sharply with the more modern all-enclosed vehicles. In Bolton ownership, these cars returned to the Farnworth route, where the conductor of car 34 turns the trolley pole at the 'Black Horse' terminus in the late 1930s. (W.A. Camwell)

Bury, too, whilst operating many all-enclosed cars, kept a number of balcony cars in service in the 1930s. Car 34, in the Haymarket, Bury, in 1935, was supplied new as a top-covered balcony car in 1904, and retained its original style to the end. (A.M. Gunn)

Oldham 44, at the Summit Inn in 1935, was an example of a 1902 tramcar with a top-cover added. Oldham operated a mixture of open-fronted, semi-vestibuled, and all-enclosed cars throughout the 1930s. Car 44 was on route 7 to Hathershaw (for Ashton) and carries a poster inviting people to have their parcels delivered by tram. (A.M. Gunn)

For the long joint service from Waterhead to Manchester, Oldham usually allocated vestibuled vehicles. In 1937, car 4 stands between a Manchester bus and tram in Stevenson Square, a terminus concealed from nearby Piccadilly. (A.M. Gunn)

The third track at Hollinwood on the Oldham–Manchester boundary was installed to allow waiting cars to stand out of the way of the through services. It remains unused as Oldham 132 to Waterhead passes 24, as the latter waits to use the crossover for its return journey to Shaw (Wren's Nest). Oldham bus 19 for Uppermill is parked on the left. (W.A. Camwell)

Manchester and Salford's joint cross-city tramway services, begun in 1926, were severed in the 1930s, allegedly because of traffic congestion. The last to survive was service 34, Weaste to Belle Vue, which ended through running on 24 July 1937. Salford bogie car 224, followed by Manchester 723, passes through Piccadilly on the last day. (A.M. Gunn)

Manchester's final design of tramcar was the single-truck high-speed 'Pullman Car' favoured by manager Stuart Pilcher and introduced in 1930–2. The 'Pilchers' had a sleek look, and car 381, standing in Brunswick Street by the University in 1938, may be compared with the standard car passing along Oxford Road in the background. (W.A. Camwell)

The last day of operation of the Ashton tramways was 1 March 1938. Open-ended cars were still in use early that day when car 33 made its last journey to Manchester's Piccadilly. In the afternoon, trolley-buses replaced the trams, which were driven off to be scrapped at Hyde Road, where Manchester's spacious permanent way yard was the last resting place of many local vehicles. It was usual to salvage any reusable material before the bodies were burnt, for which latter service Manchester charged £10 per car. (A.M. Gunn)

Stockport trams continued to be seen in the city centre on the routes from Exchange to Hazel Grove via Stockport (service 35), and from Albert Square to Stockport (Mersey Square, service 35B). Car 58 is in London Road as it approaches Piccadilly in March 1939. (A.M. Gunn)

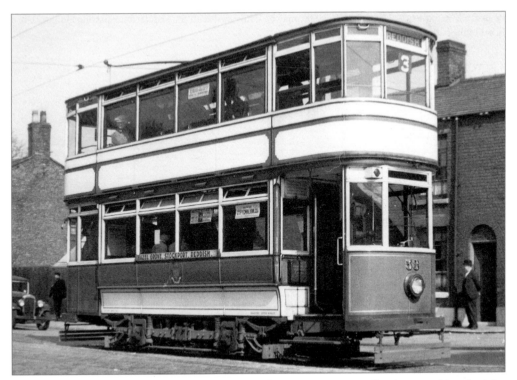

Route numbers were not usually displayed on Stockport trams, except for those working the joint services into Manchester in the 1930s when the number 35 (with A, B or C suffix as required) was hung in the end top-deck window. Routes 1 to 4 were Stockport's own services, not normally on view. Car 53 was an exception. (M.J. O'Connor)

Traffic congestion in the city centre was such that Manchester and Salford planned to convert the remaining tramway routes to motor bus operation by 1940. Deansgate in 1935, with traffic overtaking tramcars on the inside, demonstrates the hazards of boarding or alighting in busy streets. There is no doubt that trams in the centre of the roadway caused obstructions. Tram routes had already been reduced or shortened throughout the 1930s, but further abandonment was halted by the outbreak of war in 1939 and the consequent shortage of imported fuel. The remaining tram services thus enjoyed a temporary reprieve, but many of the vehicles were already almost 40 years old. (The *Guardian*)

For a short period, when invasion scares were at their height, public service vehicles ran without destination displays and with all reference to their operator obscured. The reason for this strange practice was to deny information to the enemy. It was argued that spies or parachutists landing in the area would not know where they were! Manchester tram 448 in Albert Square in 1940 has a blank destination and shows only a route number, which, it was thought, would be known only to the locals. Note also the headlamp mask, required by the blackout regulations. (*Manchester Evening News*)

The town of Bolton lies in a semicircle of the Pennine hills, and is occasionally subject to severe weather conditions. Tramcar 308 was one of several vehicles stranded in the heavy snowfall of January 1940. Tramway men often referred to the open-fronted cars as 'freezers' because of the extremely cold conditions endured by platform staff. (St Regis)

Tramway abandonments resumed in post-war years. The last SHMD tram ran in 1945, Oldham's in 1946. Salford and Bolton both finished on 31 March 1947, as replacement buses became available from manufacturers returning to peacetime production. This picture was taken at Bolton's Tonge Moor terminus on the last day of operation. (Tillotson's Newspapers)

Many tramway authorities chose to dispose of their old tramcars by first removing any parts or materials, such as metals, for which a good price might be obtained as scrap, and then towing the empty hulks to Manchester's Hyde Road for burning. In 1947, after the last route had closed, Bolton opted to break up the trams in its own premises. (St Regis)

Manchester's last tramcars ran on 10 January 1949. On the previous day Stockport cars ran a special tour to Exchange, where car 67 was photographed alongside a Manchester tram. Manchester's 38 Pilcher cars went on to service elsewhere; the rest were burnt. Bury trams also ended in 1949, leaving only Stockport to carry on until 1951. (R.B. Parr)

TROLLEY BUSES

The trolley bus could be regarded as a cross between a tram and a bus. It needed overhead wires, but no track. Among the pioneers of trolley bus operation in the area were Stockport, Ramsbottom, and Wigan, but none developed into full systems. The initial advantage over the tramway was that expensive track investment was not required. In 1913 Ramsbottom Urban District Council (to the north of Bury) commenced a 'Trackless Electric Tramcar' service on a route between Edenfield and Holcombe Brook via Ramsbottom station. It lasted until 1931. Only three vehicles were bought, of which no. 2 is seen here at Edenfield.

Stockport's trolley buses also commenced in 1913, shortly before the Ramsbottom service. Stockport's three vehicles drew current via a German device, a flexible trolley (known unofficially as the 'monkey'), running on a single pair of overhead wires. When vehicles travelling in opposite directions met, trolleys were unhooked and exchanged.

The Stockport trolleys worked a 2 mile route from the town centre to Offerton until 1920. The system was not extended. Neighbouring authorities were suspicious, and spares became difficult to obtain in the war years. In addition, 'monkeys' had been known to fall from the wires when turning. Bus 3 is seen on the first day of operation.

Next to experiment with the trolley bus was Wigan, where in 1925 four single-deckers were used to replace trams on one route. In an area plagued by mining subsidence, trackless vehicles were attractive, but on the abandonment of the tramways in 1931 it was not thought worthwhile to maintain electric traction for only one short route.

Oldham co-operated with Ashton in a brief venture in 1925–6, from which Oldham soon withdrew, but Ashton persisted and in 1938 entered into an arrangement with Manchester which lasted until the end of trolley bus operation in 1966. Ashton 79, built by Crossley in 1950, in navy blue, cream and red livery, is seen here in 1954 in Manchester.

The South Lancashire Company was the most ambitious trolley bus operator in the region, converting tramcar routes to trolley bus operation in 1930–3. The Atherton to Farnworth route through Worsley and Swinton, 14 miles long, had termini only 5 miles apart. Trolley 45, TJ 3334 a 1933 Guy chassis with Roe bodywork, was photographed in Worsley in 1957. (E. Gray)

Short-workings on the Atherton–Farnworth route were regular features, and a reversing triangle was provided for vehicles turning back at Swinton. Trolley bus 36 (TJ 3325) was captured in the snow at Swinton in February 1955. (E. Gray)

Worsley, 1957, as SLT trolley 24 (TF 5803) pauses on its journey from Atherton to Swinton. This was one of 30 large three-axle vehicles, built by Guy Motors in 1931, but fitted with a new, modernised front-end, giving a smoother profile. (E.Gray)

Seen from the rear, the same 1931 vehicle betrays its date of origin, for, whilst several other vehicles received a full modernising treatment to side and rear panelling, 24's 1955 face-lift was not extended to the back end. The photograph was taken at Worsley Delph, 1957. (E. Gray)

SLT 6-wheeled trolley bus 28 (TF 5807) was another vehicle which received only a new front, with no alterations to its sides and rear. This is Swinton Depot forecourt, in the last year of operation, 1958. (E. Gray)

SLT 52 (BTE 951) was one of ten Leyland trolley buses with Roe highbridge bodies, delivered in 1936–8. The rear view, in Bolton bus station, 1956, emphasises the length of the trolley booms. When Bolton trams ceased to work to Four Lane Ends, four of these vehicles (48–51) were purchased by Bolton but operated by SLT (in SLT livery) on the Bolton–Leigh service. (E. Gray)

Manchester's investment in trolley buses was not made until 1938. The General Manager preferred to replace trams with motor buses, but when conversion of the Ashton routes was imminent, he accepted with reluctance the council's desire to use home-produced electricity rather than imported oil. Consequently, 38 four-wheelers (numbered 1000–1037) and 38 larger six-wheelers (1050–1087) were purchased and the new Rochdale Road Depot was built to house them. The chassis were a mixture of Leyland and Crossley products, but Crossley supplied all the bodies, and all had Metropolitan Vickers electrical equipment. Bus 1051 is seen on tilt test. (MCT)

A wartime view of Manchester six-wheeler 1076 on route 29 at Ashton Market Place, shows it with trolley booms fastened down, apparently deserted by its crew. Note the headlamp masks and white fenders of the blackout period. The pre-war livery with the cream swoops gave a streamlined effect.

Trolley bus 1032 threads its way between buses and trams in Piccadilly in the immediate post-war period, November 1946. Note the obtrusive overhead equipment. Whereas tramcars were earthed into the track, and therefore required only a single wire, the trolley buses needed an extra overhead line for that purpose.

Manchester's final addition to the trolley bus system was the Hyde route in 1950, begun months after tramcar services had ceased, the conversion delayed because of slow delivery of new vehicles. Trolley 1210, new in 1948–9, stands at the Piccadilly terminus of the Hyde route in 1955. Trolley bus operation in Manchester ended in December 1966. (E. Gray)

MOTOR BUSES,
1940–1969

Crossley single-deck bus no. 50 (AXJ 466), 1940. Wartime oil shortages led to the experimental adaptation of buses fuelled by ordinary town gas, which was stored in bags on the roof. Manchester ran two such vehicles in 1940–2. Twenty other vehicles were equipped with 'producer gas' trailers in 1942–4. (MCT)

A 1938 Crossley Mancunian 683 (ENA 719) in the yard of Manchester's Hyde Road Depot, displays its streamlined livery as adapted to conform to the wartime blackout regulations in 1940. Its roof has been darkened, and white paint has been applied to mudguards, rear corners, and dog rails. The offside headlamp has been covered with a mask allowing only thin slits of light to show through, whilst the nearside lamp has been removed altogether. (MCT)

Wartime shortages of paint sometimes led to the cream portions being replaced by the more easily obtainable battleship grey. Manchester Leyland 912 (FNF 812), seen in Boyle Street at the side of Queens Road Depot, has been treated in this manner. The more durable red has been merely varnished. It was feared that white roofs might show up to enemy aircraft, and these, too, were painted grey. (MCT)

In 1939–40 Manchester took deliveries of new vehicles, and was thus able to lend buses to towns which suffered wartime losses. Leyland 949 (FXJ 980) of 1940 remained in the fleet for over 20 years. It carries the plainer post-war livery, adopted as an economy measure, with the title of the undertaking altered to 'City of Manchester'. (MCT)

The supply of new vehicles during and immediately after the war was strictly controlled by the Government. In 1946 Bolton was allowed to purchase Crossleys built to the Ministry's restrictive standards of the time. An example undergoes the tilt test at Cravens body builders.

Bolton Crossley 311 (BWH 125) was a 1946 utility acquisition, which remained in service until 1961. Behind it is Leyland 339, with Crossley body of 1947, at Howell Croft in about 1962. The clock of Bolton's Town Hall is visible on the skyline. (E. Gray)

Snow in Bolton again. Single-deck Crossley (either 6 or 7, DBN 976–7, of 1949) was temporarily abandoned in this snowdrift which blocked the route to Affetside, a district between Bolton and Bury.

The North Western Road Car Company fitted many new bodies to refurbished chassis. Bristol 828 (JA 7728) of 1938, received a new Willowbrook body in 1952, and had the suffix A added to its number. The photograph was taken at Lower Mosley Street bus station, Manchester. (R.F. Mack)

In the late 1950s Rochdale Corporation purchased AEC Regent buses with Weymann bodies, many of which remained in service for some 20 years. The livery was an attractive blue and cream. Bus 212 (GDK 712) waits in Rochdale town centre before leaving on the Littleborough route. (E. Gray)

After abandoning its trams in 1951, Stockport tended to order most of its bus fleet from Leyland, but the local firm of Crossley was patronised on occasions. Crossley 262 (CJA 786), in the standard red and cream livery, stands in Mersey Square, Stockport, in 1954. (E. Gray)

In 1943–5 Ashton-under-Lyne's fleet was augmented with 16 Guy buses, whose wartime 'utility' bodies were replaced as soon as circumstances permitted. In 1955 bus 74 (left) had recently received a new body in the revised livery of 'peacock blue' and cream. Buses 41 and 68 had Crossley bodies of 1951–2 in the old livery. (E. Gray)

In post-war years, Lancashire United Transport regularly purchased chassis from Guy Motors of Wolverhampton. Bus 191 (KTB 104) was a Guy Arab II with Roe bodywork, new in 1949, and seen on the cross-country express service to Newcastle. Guy's 'Indian Chief' radiator cap was a well-known trade mark. (R.F. Mack)

Lancashire United double-deck bus 20 (115 JTD), a Guy Arab IV with Northern Counties body, was new in 1959. It is seen in its last year of operation, 1975, in Liverpool Road, Peel Green, on the joint service to Warrington. By this date, one-man operation was well established, and rear-entrance buses were becoming a rarity. (E. Gray)

From 1952 until the early 1960s, the Salford City Transport fleet consisted mainly of 8 ft wide Daimler chassis fitted with Gardner engines from the local Patricroft works. Salford had a post-war change of livery from red and cream to green and cream, with silver roof. Bus 407 is pictured here at Piccadilly, Manchester. (R.F. Mack)

For reasons of economy, several transport undertakings changed to a simpler, spray-painted livery. Bury abandoned its earlier colour scheme in favour of light green and cream. Some rear-entrance buses remained in use to the end of municipal operation, but the leading vehicle, dating from 1958, has platform doors. This is Bury Market Place, 1969. (E. Gray)

From 1937 to 1952 the SHMD Joint Board bought only Daimler chassis. This 1948 example (no. 40, KMA 510), rebodied by Northern Counties in 1954, is shown working a rural area route in 1962. In its original form it had been one of six municipal Daimlers demonstrated at the 1948 British Trade Exhibition in Denmark. (SHMD)

Wigan Market Place in the 1960s, with a collection of Leyland vehicles. As would be expected, Wigan patronised the local firm of Massey Brothers for many of its bus bodies. Compare this with the picture at the same location on page 58. (Greater Manchester Transport)

One-man operation gained popularity and eventually became the norm in the 1960s. The passengers' forward view in Bolton single-deck bus 12 (UWH 322) in 1962 includes advice (top right) on how to check details on tickets issued by machine. (Bolton Transport)

The last Leyland front-engined bus for the home market was delivered in 1969, by which date most, but not all, transport undertakings in the Manchester area had acquired double-deck buses of the rear-engined type, with forward entrance suitable for one-man operation. This example of the new breed was new to Bolton in 1965. (Bolton Transport)

PASSENGER TRANSPORT EXECUTIVE, DE-REGULATION & METROLINK

Proposals for a unified transport system in the Greater Manchester area had been made as early as 1931. Nothing resulted until the Government's 1968 Transport Act provided for the creation of a Passenger Transport Authority. In 1969 the assets of existing operators, which included over 3,000 vehicles, were transferred to the South East Lancashire & North East Cheshire (SELNEC, later Greater Manchester Transport) Passenger Transport Executive, a new organisation charged with the task of providing an integrated and efficient system of services in the whole region. One of the first vehicles to be repainted in the new livery of 'sunglow orange and cream' was this ex-Bolton Daimler. (E. Gray)

Under new ownership, buses were renumbered fairly quickly, but the repainting programme lasted several years. Thus the varied colours of the former undertakings remained in evidence. This ex-Rochdale AEC (NDK 980) in the new livery survived long enough to be purchased for preservation and restored to the former Rochdale blue. (E. Gray)

Under the new administration, many vehicles of the former municipal fleets were redistributed to work from 'foreign' garages. In Oldham's Mumps Depot in 1975 were a large number of ex-Stockport Leylands, with ill-fitting destination blinds for Oldham routes, mixing with the more traditional inhabitants. (E. Gray)

Many former Salford vehicles were re-allocated to depots in Manchester, Oldham, Stalybridge and Wigan. An ex-Salford bus passes a vehicle still in Manchester red in Albert Square, 1974. Its large and highly visible destination aperture has been partly obscured in order to accommodate the smaller Manchester-style standard blind. (E. Gray)

Lloyd Road, Levenshulme, 1979. This ex-Salford Leyland bus was one of several allocated to Manchester's Birchfields Road Depot, where staff left the destination window unobscured, allowing two lines of the new narrow blind to show, and leaving passengers to guess which was the more correct. (E. Gray)

Leigh, the smallest constituent member of the new Passenger Transport Executive, operated some low-bridge buses, with sunken gangway on the top deck, because of restricted-height railway bridges in its area. The last journey of a low-bridge bus in Greater Manchester was that of ex-Leigh 779 YTB on 6 July 1977. (Greater Manchester Transport)

Lloyd Road, Levenshulme, 1977. An ex-Leigh AEC Renown, re-allocated to Birchfields Depot, works the 262 route to Eccles, formerly numbered 22. As the third digit could not be displayed, the crew sensibly decided to opt for the old service number. GMT standard bus 7055 stands on the left. (E. Gray)

'De-regulation' of bus services attracted new operators. One of the first was the Lyntown Bus Company, based in Eccles. Working with single-deck Bristol Reliances, new routes were pioneered, but copied by GMT, causing the proprietor to revert to private hire business only. Bus 5, WSV 552, is at Peel Green, April 1987. (E. Gray)

In September 1987 two businessmen formed a short-lived Blue Bus Company, and began a two-hourly service on a Manchester to Culcheth route, using first an ex-Eastern Scottish bus, but then in December acquiring a London Routemaster (WLT 572) on loan, still in full London Transport livery. It is seen here at Peel Green, January 1978. (E. Gray)

A local hotelier began a series of short routes under the title 'Eccles Greys', using five Ford 16-seater mini-buses (B410–414 NJF). The new services linked shopping centres, hospitals and housing estates away from the main traffic arteries. B411 NJF is seen in Eccles bus station during the first week of operation, February 1988. (E. Gray)

Operators attracted to the area in 1988 included Ribble, from the northern side, and Crosville, the latter running to Eccles from Cheshire. At Peel Green in January 1988, this Crosville bus lacked the blinds necessary to display the correct destination. Both Ribble and Crosville made use of hastily prepared destination boards stuck in front windows. (E. Gray)

Shearings (later Timeline) inaugurated a cross-Manchester route from Peel Green to East Didsbury. Bus 93 (KOM 793P), boasting a digital destination display, stands in front of a standard GMT bus in New Lane, Peel Green, on the first day of the new service, 11 January 1988. Competition between rival operators was keen. A Shearing's driver was heard announcing to waiting passengers that he was 'going the same way as the other lot'. GMT appeared to make an unnecessary confusion of the de-regulation process, with re-allocation of service numbers and changes of terminal points. The dependable and familiar pattern of routes was largely lost. Despite the stated desire to woo travellers from the private car, frequent alterations to routes and timetables have made it difficult for members of the public to keep abreast of changes, and have prevented the development of a stable and reliable network. (E. Gray)

GMT standard bus 6974 on the Bolton route, 1987. Some competitors succumbed when GMT duplicated services and thus divided the number of passengers per operator. Opposition gone, after a period of sole operation, GMT would discover that some routes were unremunerative, and withdraw the service, leaving bus-less citizens to wonder why GMT bothered to compete. (E. Gray)

Unit 1022, Sale station, 1995. Manchester regained a tramway in 1992, when Metrolink constructed a length of city centre track (with a short branch to Piccadilly 'Undercroft') linking the electric railways to Bury and Altrincham. Use of the former railway lines required high-access vehicles to fit existing station platforms. The 26 two-car units (1001–1026) were built in Italy. (E. Gray)

A ramp lifts the street track at the side of the former Central station (now 'G-Mex' exhibition centre) to a new 'bow-string' bridge over Great Bridgewater Street, thus gaining access to the Altrincham line. The bridge, manufactured in Belgium, is designed 'to reflect its surroundings'. Unit 1016 crosses, 1995. (E. Gray)

Unit 1008, St Peter's Square, 1995. The street section of Metrolink has obtrusive, plentiful, and unnecessarily robust poles to support the overhead wires. These, together with high pavement platforms, signs, ticket machines, and shelters (of French manufacture, 'architecturally correct . . . to blend in with the cityscape') give an impression of untidy clutter. (E. Gray)

The Manchester Tramway Museum Society runs preserved tramcar 765 on a length of track in Heaton Park. Dating from 1914, the car was withdrawn from service in 1930, its body surviving unprotected as a farm outhouse. Purchased and rescued in 1960, the car has been restored to operational condition by volunteers. (E. Gray)

ACKNOWLEDGEMENTS

The author has nursed an interest in local transport matters for over 50 years. During that time he has received much help in the way of information and photographs from other interested parties, both inside and outside the transport industry. The sources of some of the illustrations were not always noted at the time, and although pictures are individually acknowledged where the photographer is known, apologies must be offered for any inadvertent omissions. The author is particularly grateful to the late W.A. Camwell, Walter Gratwicke, R.F. Mack, Maurice O'Connor, and R.B. Parr, all of whom kindly gave help in the past and granted permission for their work to be reproduced, as did J.R. Carter, Gordon Coltas (Locofotos), W.D. Cooper, and A.M. Gunn. For general help in the search for illustrations the author is grateful to the National Railway Museum at York; the Manchester Ship Canal Company; and Arthur Haynes. Photographs credited to MCT come from the files of the former Manchester Corporation Transport Department, rescued and cared for by the late G.R. Dunning. Alan Palmer of Worsley kindly drew the map (reproduced on page 23) showing railway termini in central Manchester.

The railway companies and many of the road transport undertakings in the Greater Manchester region have been the subject of individual detailed histories, and for much information used in captions the author has consulted the published works of writers Paul Bolger (Cheshire lines); D.M. Eyre & C.W. Heaps (Manchester buses); Brian Haresnape (Fowler and Stanier locomotives); W.G.S. Hyde (Ashton and MBRO); E.M. Johnson (Manchester railways); A.K. Kirby (Manchester tramways); John Marshall (Lancashire & Yorkshire Railway); Maurice Marshall (Stockport tramways); Eric Ogden (North Western and Lancashire United Transport); E.K. Stretch (Wigan and South Lancashire tramways); D. Thorpe (Ship Canal railways); and Ian Yearsley (Manchester tramways). Their skills and the thoroughness of their researches are acknowledged with admiration and gratitude. Publicity material issued by the Passenger Transport Executive, British Rail, Greater Manchester Buses, and Metrolink has provided information (and much innocent amusement) on more recent and current developments.

Members of the Manchester Transport Museum Society and the Greater Manchester Transport Society have shared the author's interests in local transport developments over the years, and their friendship and support has been valued. The unfailing courtesy and advice of Simon Fletcher (Alan Sutton Publishing) has been greatly appreciated, and finally, thanks are recorded to the author's wife, Kathleen, without whom nothing would be achieved, and whose tolerance and encouragement have been essential to the completion of this work.

BRITAIN IN OLD PHOTOGRAPHS

LONDON

Acton T & A Harper-Smith
Around Whetstone J Heathfield
Barnes, Mortlake and Sheen P Loobey
Balham and Tooting P Loobey
Brixton and Norwood J Dudman
Crystal Palace, Penge and Anerley
  M Scott
Ealing and Northfield R Essen
Greenwich and Woolwich K D Clark
Hackney: A Second Selection D Mander
Hammersmith and Shepherds Bush
  J Farrell & C Bayliss
Hampstead to Primrose Hill M Holmes
Fairey Aircraft R Sturdivant
Islington D Withet & V Hart
Kensington and Chelsea B Denny &
  C Starren
Lewisham and Deptford: A Second
  Selection J Coulter
Marylebone and Paddington R Bowden
Royal Arsenal, The, Woolwich
  R Masters
Southwark S Humphrey
Stepney R Taylor & C Lloyd
Stoke Newington M Manley
Streatham P Loobey
Theatrical London P Berry
Uxbridge, Hillingdon and Cowley
  K Pearce
Wimbledon P Loobey
Woolwich B Evans

MONMOUTHSHIRE

Chepstow and the River Wye A
  Rainsbury
Monmouth and the River Wye
  Ed. Monmouth Musuem

NORFOLK

Cromer & District M Warren
Great Yarmouth M Teun
Norfolk at War N Storey
North Walsham & District N Storey
Wymondham and Attleborough P Yaxley

NORTHAMPTONSHIRE

Around Stony Stratford A Lambert

NOTTINGHAMSHIRE

Arnold and Bestwood M Spick
Arnold and Bestwood II M Spick
Around Newark T Warner
Changing Face of Nottingham, The
  G Oldfield
Kirkby and District F Ashley et al
Mansfield Old Mansfield Society
Newark T Warner
Nottingham Yesterday and Today
  G Oldfield
Sherwood Forest D Ottewell
Vale of Belvoir T Hickman
Victorian Nottingham M Payne

OXFORDSHIRE

Around Abingdon P Horn
Around Didcot and the Hagbournes
  B Lingham

Around Henley-on-Thames S Ellis
Around Highworth & Faringdon
  G Tanner
Around Wallingford D Beasley
Around Wheatley M Gunther
Around Witney C Mitchell
Around Woodstock J Bond
Banburyshire S Gray
Burford A Jewell
Garsington M Guntner
Oxford: The University J Rhodes
Oxfordshire Railways: A Second
  Selection L Waters
Thame To Watlington N Hood
Wantage, Faringdon and the Vale
  Villages N Hood
Witney T Worley
Witney District T Worley

POWYS

Brecon Brecknock Museum
Welshpool E Bredsdorff

SHROPSHIRE

RAF Cosford A Brew
Shrewsbury D Trumper
Shrewsbury: A Second Selection
  D Trumper
Whitchurch to Market Drayton
  M Morris

SOMERSET / AVON

Around Keynsham and Saltford B Lowe
Around Taunton N Chipchase
Around Weston-Super-Mare S Poole
Bath J Hudson
Bridgwater and the River Parrett
  R Fitzhugh
Bristol D Moorcroft
The Changing Face of Keynsham B Lowe
  & M Whitehead
Chard and Ilminster G Gosling
Crewkerne and the Ham Stone Villages
  G Gosling
Frome D Gill
Mendips, The C Howell
Midsomer Norton and Radstock
  C Howell
Minehead J Astell
Somerton and Langport G Gosling
Taunton N Chipchase
Wells C Howell
Weston-Super-Mare S Poole

STAFFORDSHIRE

Around Leek R Poole
Around Rugeley T Randall
Around Stafford J Anslow
Around Tamworth R Sulima
Around Tettenhall and Codsall M Mills
Black Country Railways N Williams
Black Country Road Transport J Boulton
Black Country Transport: Aviation
  A Brew
Brierley Hill S Hill
Bushbury A Chatwin
Heywood J Hudson
Lichfield H Clayton

Pattingham and Wombourne M Mills
Sedgley and District T Genge
Smethwick J Maddison
Stafford J Anslow & T Randall
Staffordshire Railways M Hitches
Stoke-on-Trent I Lawley
Tipton J Brimble & K Hodgkins
Walsall D Gilbert
Wednesbury I Bott
West Bromwich R Pearson

SUFFOLK

Around Mildenhall C Dring
Around Woodbridge H Phelps
Ipswich: A Second Selection D Kindred
Lowestoft I Robb
Southwold to Aldeburgh H Phelps
Stowmarket B Malster
Suffolk at Work: Farming and Fishing
  B Malster

SURREY

Around Epsom P Berry
Cheam And Belmont P Berry
Croydon S Bligh
Farnham: A Second Selection J Parratt
Kingston T Everson
Richmond Ed. Richmond Local
  History Society
Sutton P Berry

SUSSEX

Around Crawley M Goldsmith
Around Haywards Heath J Middleton
Around Heathfield A Gillet
Around Heathfield: A Second Selection
  A Gillet
Around Worthing S White
Arundel and the Arun Valley J D Godfrey
Bishopstone and Seaford P Pople
Bishopstone and Seaford: A Second
  Selection P Pople & P Berry
Brighton and Hove J Middleton
Brighton and Hove: A Second Selection
  J Middleton
Crawley New Town P Allen & J Green
East Grinstead N Dunnachie
Hastings P Haines
Hastings: A Second Selection P Haines
High Weald, The B Harwood
High Weald: A Second Selection
  B Harwood
Horsham and District T Wales
Lancing and Sompting P Fry
Lewes J Middleton
RAF Tangmere A Saunders

TAYSIDE

Dundee at Work J Murray

WARWICKSHIRE

Along the Avon from Stratford to
  Tewkesbury J Jeremiah
Around Coventry D McGrory
Around Leamington Spa J Cameron
Around Leamington Spa II J Cameron
Around Warwick R Booth
Bedworth J Burton

Birmingham Railways M Hitches
Coventry: A Second Selection D McGrory
Nuneaton S Clews
Rugby Rugby Local History
  Research Group
Stourbridge R Clarke

WESTMORLAND

Kendal M Duff

WILTSHIRE

Around Amesbury P Daniels
Around Devizes D Buxton
Around Highworth G Tanner
Around Highworth & Faringdon
  G Tanner
Around Melksham Ed. Melksham and
  District Historical Association
Around Salisbury P Daniels
Around Wilton P Daniels
Around Wootton Bassett, Cricklade and
  Purton T Sharp
Castle Combe to Malmesbury A Wilson
Chippenham and Lacock A Wilson
Corsham & Box A Wilson
Marlborough: A Second Selection
  P Colman
Nadder Valley R Sawyer
Salisbury P Saunders
Salisbury: A Second Selection P Daniels
Salisbury: A Third Selection P Daniels
Swindon: A Third Selection Ed. The
  Swindon Society
Swindon: A Fifth Selection B Bridgeman
Trowbridge M Marshman

WORCESTERSHIRE

Around Malvern K Smith
Around Pershore M Dowty
Around Worcester R Jones
Evesham to Bredon F Archer
Redditch and the Needle District
  R Saunders
Redditch: A Second Selection
  R Saunders
Tenbury Wells D Green
Worcester M Dowty
Worcester in a Day M Dowty
Worcestershire at Work R Jones

YORKSHIRE

Around Rotherham A Munford
Around Thirsk J Harding & P Wyon
Beverley P Deans & J Markham
Bridlington I & M Sumner
Holderness I & M Sumner
Huddersfield: A Second Selection
  H Wheeler
Huddersfield: A Third Selection
  H Wheeler
Leeds Road and Rail R Vickers
Otley & District P Wood
Pudsey Pudsey Civic Society
Scarborough D Coggins
Skipton and the Dales Ed. Friends of
  Craven Museum
Wakefield C Johnstone
Yorkshire Wolds, The I & M Sumner

To order any of these titles please telephone our distributor, Littlehampton Book Services on 01903 721596

For a catalogue of these and our other titles please ring Regina Schinner on 01453 731114